Sell Beer! How to Start a Microbrewery from the Ground Up

Microbrewery, Nanobrewery, Taproom, Pub, Brewhouse, Bar

Make and Sell Custom Craft Beer, IPA, Small Batch Brews

By

Stanley Harper

Copyrighted Material

*Copyright © 2021 – **CSB Academy Publishing Company***

All Rights Reserved.

Without limiting the rights under the copyright laws, no part of this publication may be reproduced, stored in or introduced into a retrieval system, or transmitted, in any form or by any means (electronic, mechanical, photocopying, recording or otherwise), without the prior written consent of the publisher of this book.

CSB Academy Publishing Company publishes its books and guides in a variety of electronic and print formats, Some content that appears in print may not be available in electronic format, and vice versa.

CSB Academy Publishing Co.

Cover Design

By

Stephanie Martin

First Edition

Contents

Introduction *6*

The Backstory of Craft Beer *9*
    Craft Vs. Mainstream 10
    The Craft Beer Industry 12
        Success Stories 15

Microbrewery vs. Craft Brewery *18*
    Types of Small Breweries 20
    What's a Brewpub? 23
    Taproom Breweries 25
    Farm Breweries 26

The Basics of Beer Making *28*
    Easy Home Brewing 29
    Beer Making, Step-by-Step 34

Our Story: Starting Out *40*

The Business Plan *43*

Market Research and Consumer Analysis *47*
    Niche Markets 51

Location *53*

Equipment 57

Finances and Start-up Costs *62*

What to Consider with Financial Planning 64

    Working Capital 68

    Keys to Healthy Finances 69

Funding 72

Lager Laws *77*

Legal Identity, Business Name, and Trademark 81

Brewer's Notice in the TTB 85

Brewer's Bond 86

Other Licenses 88

    Restaurant liquor and all liquor license 88

    Beer and wine liquor license 89

    Tavern license 89

    Server license 89

Insurance 91

Sell, Sell, Sell: Branding *93*

Branding and Logos 93

    Who 104

    What 104

    Where 105

    When 105

    Why 106

Logo Design 108

Vision and Mission Statement 110

    What is a Vision Statement? 111

    Vision Statement vs. Mission Statement 112

    What Shapes Your Vision? 112

Using a Vision Statement 113

    Writing a Vision Statement 114

What is a Mission Statement? 119

Packaging Matters 119

Marketing Strategies 126

All About Scaling *136*

Distribution 136

Staffing and Boosting Morale 141

    Hiring Your First Employee 144

    Training Employees 146

    The Real Cost of an Employee 147

    Employer Responsibilities 149

Final Thoughts *150*

Introduction

Who doesn't love a good beer? I mean, I certainly do – and it's not just because my father used to take me out around town whenever I'd have troubles (and I had a lot of troubles – believe me). It may not have been much of a bonding moment, two grown men drinking away their sorrows in a sad little bar downtown. But while there wasn't anything fancy about the dim overhead lights and the cheap vinyl tiles, all that really mattered to me was my old man and me sitting there like lifelong buddies, like we were meant to do this forever until the end of time.

Of course, nothing good ever lasts, and my father isn't immortal (although I wish he were). When he passed away quietly in his sleep, it was one of those middle-of-the-night calls you always wish you'd never get. It's that dread of the phone ringing in the wee hours of the morning and the sinking feeling that you somehow know it's bad news.

I never really did get over it, his passing. But while some people might wallow in grief and self-pity, I found a different outlet to honor my dad's memory – starting my own microbrewery. What better way to keep his spirit (heh, spirit) alive than by keeping the tradition he and I both loved so much?

Now, my wife and I haven't always had the most business-savvy of minds, and when this all began, we were just a couple of wide-eyed newbies eager to follow our passions. Of course, while they always tell you to follow your dreams and reach for the stars and all that, life isn't all sunshine and butterflies. Passion can only get you so far, and the cold, harsh truth of reality is that to succeed, you need an actual plan if you don't want to end up miserable and broke.

With all that said, and after building my own micro beer brewery from the ground up, I've decided to share everything I know to make sure you don't fall into the same traps I fell into when I was first starting out. This isn't a how-to for brewing beer, mind you – you'd pretty much already have that down pat if you're a real aficionado. Instead, what I'd like to do with this book is to show you the ropes and guide you through the business side of things, and no, you don't really need a Business degree to make it out of this commercial world unscathed.

So, if you gain anything from this book, which I hope you do, or if you have feedback to offer, do me a favor and leave a review where you purchased this book online? Online reviews give me valuable insight into how to improve. Thanks a lot!

The Backstory of Craft Beer

All great things start with a great idea, and a great business idea can change your life. That's pretty much what happened with craft beer. To help you come up with your own great idea, business and marketing people will often advise you to find a niche in the market – a unique area of specialization that isn't already done to death. Ideally, you can carve one out for yourself if you can't find one. No matter how small of a hole or crack you find, wedge and shimmy yourself in there and build on your own unique, awesome idea. Do it well, and serve the needs of your market. Find your idea, then you'll find your people.

Craft Vs. Mainstream

The craft beer industry started out this way back in the late 2000s as a small niche for beer enthusiasts – well, it really started in the 1980s, but the ball didn't start rolling until the late 2000s – when everything in the beer market was owned by goliaths that monopolized the entire beer industry. Back then, most of the beer you probably drank in the US was made by Anheuser-Busch and MillerCoors. These 2 behemoths dominated nearly 90% of the beer productions in the US.

Fast forward to today: Beer sales are declining, with the entire beer market dropping by 2%, but it seems like it's not the case for craft beers. Sales for craft beer back in 2019 were surging, and the domestic sales of craft beer made up 24% of the whole US beer market, totaling a whopping 27.6 billion dollars. It's no wonder "Big Beer" has been quietly buying up independent craft breweries. It's only natural for them to want a piece of the action too.

Nowadays, manufacturers are looking for ways to cut down labor costs and make everything more efficient. This means less manpower and, at the same time, an increase in output. But the opposite is happening in the craft beer industry – microbreweries like us, not only in the US but all around the world, are painstakingly honing their craft, so much so that to produce a barrel of craft beer requires more people than a large corporate-scale brewery normally would. They do it for the money – we do it for our undying love for beer. Cheers! We call it the "craft beer revolution" – a made-in-America economic triumph against beer conglomerates that all started when consumer demands inevitably shifted.

Recently, consumers – the bulk of which are millennials – have been very vocal about receiving quality products in exchange for their hard-earned cash. They want more choices. They want to live healthier, more meaningful lives.

There's also a growing awareness about the impact of their everyday choices and an increasing call to support local and small businesses – taking pride in buying locally made and handcrafted goods – although this trend is bound to change again since the Gen-Z's are now coming of age (more on that later). But unlike the previous generations, they won't just settle for what's being served; they want more. Some established corporations are failing to serve this need, and a lot of small-time local entrepreneurs are stepping up to the plate. As an example, you can see this not only in the rise of microbreweries but also in the death of fast-fashion retailers and the rapid growth of fast-casual restaurants.

By jumping on this growing demand, microbreweries like myself focused on niches that the larger breweries have ignored for years, like the IPAs or the Indian Pale Ales – these make up a huge portion of what microbreweries are serving. Right now, there are approximately 7,450 craft breweries in the U.S. In your town, there are probably a handful or more of smaller breweries already operating.

The Craft Beer Industry

Earning money from your passion is a dream for ordinary folks like us. Only a few people in the world can proudly say that they're earning their keep by doing what they really love. We really love beer, and after quitting my day job as an adman like my father before me, we wanted a way to turn our passion for beer into a new business venture.

But as you can see, the craft beer industry, although young, is already a very crowded market. In fact, according to the numbers crunched out by the Brewers Association, there are fewer brewery openings during the past year, and it's not just because of the pandemic. The numbers have been steadily going down since 2019. The closings, on the other hand, kind of stagnated for 2020 – according to their predictions, the numbers will rise in 2021, matching the market reality pre-pandemic.

Worried? You shouldn't be because craft beer in itself has a 3 to 4% growth trend each year, and hopefully, it will get back on track in 2022. The main takeaway is that even if the market for craft beer is already crowded, hundreds of breweries are still opening each year despite the downturn of numbers. I feel like it's also worth mentioning that craft beers are a hit in cities not just here in the US but all around the world too.

High-end bars and pubs in world cities now proudly serve craft beers, and patrons are loving it. Exclusive and trendy restaurants used to pair expensive wines to complement their dishes; now, it's also paired with craft beer brewed in-house, locally, or imported in small batches just for that reason.

So naturally, the competition between breweries is getting fierce, and brewing your own batch of beer that your ever-supportive friends and colleagues love is not a surefire way to secure a slot in the microbrewery world.

Don't get me wrong – the craft beer industry is not a dog-eat-dog world by any means; in fact, it's a downright unusually friendly and helpful community that goes against the grain of our capitalist economy. We work together and share our passion for beer, but that doesn't guarantee a secure microbrewery business. Sure, we are willing to help and share our knowledge, but you must know a thing or two on how to handle your own business and stand out.

Right now, you might think of yourself as a beer connoisseur, and you brew small beloved batches in your basement. Your friends love it, and colleagues at work praise you for it. So you're thinking, why not quit your 9-to-5 and start a beer brewery? You make beer, you drink it, you sell it, they love it, you earn money. Everybody wins, right? That's why you're slugging through this book of mine. But let's face it – your drive and love for beer alone will not get you through this endeavor intact if you don't know a thing about running a business.

Success Stories

Breweries are getting more and more creative with what they want to serve customers – releasing new flavors and using years of experience honing their techniques in order to stay in the game and come out on top. You see, craft beer is already a niche, but even within the brewery world, there are even smaller niches.

Water, malt, hops, yeast: those are the four main ingredients to brewing great beer. But your business's end result will largely depend on your beer's quality and the unique spin you can give to it, which is the craftsmanship and the uniqueness of your beer. In this, niche breweries do a great job of standing out from the craft beer crowd.

This way, your fledgling brewery has a chance to stay in the market and won't be just a statistic in the Brewers Association's "closings."

Let's see some examples: in Austin, Texas, Blue Owl Brewing specializes in the sour mashing technique that gives your regular beers a unique spin that helps them stand out. Sour beers, on the other hand, is the ticket for the Crooked Stave Artisan Beer Project in Colorado, bringing them to win the 2019 GABF gold medal for Belgian-stye Lambic. Cascade Brewing in Oregon chose to devote their time and effort to serving barrel-aged beers, making them a household name for fans of sours and barrel-aged beers all over. You see now how niches play a huge role in the game?

In the end, breweries all over will try hard to stand out, but uniqueness and quality are altogether different things. Sure, your brews are unique. You make them with exotic ingredients or strange techniques, but will it taste good? Will it make your patrons come back for more and rave about it to their other friends and on their social media? Making your beers unique can make you stand out and bring them through your brewery's door, but it's the quality and the taste that will make them come back.

As my dad always told me, don't be a one-hit-wonder. The novelty will bring you immediate fame and money but just hinging on it alone will not help your business flourish. It's bringing to the table consistently and quality (delicious!) beers that will help you build your brewery, brand, and following.

But we mustn't forget the business side of things. Your ability to manage a business will push your brewery up and out of the sea of brewery startups. It's true -not everyone can brew good beer, but there's also no shortage of good brewers out there either. So it's best to remember that a good business person at the helm of any startup – because your brewery is also a startup, don't forget – is the key difference between a failed and a profitable one.

Microbrewery vs. Craft Brewery

Crafting your own beer is equal parts art and science, but starting a brewery is also – at the same time – a business. You will need lots of planning and research conducted ahead of time, so it's not just about brewing beer; you need to have a plan of action and a clear view of how you'll approach your new venture. Let's say you already have your recipe down pat. You have been brewing great-tasting beers in your garage for years now, and you feel like you are ready for your next step. What next? Do you want to start a microbrewery? A gastropub? How about a taproom brewery?

No idea what the difference is? We'll get into more details in a minute, but there are several differences between a microbrewery and a craft brewery. Basically, a microbrewery is limited to 15,000 barrels of beer per year and selling mostly outside of the brewery. A craft brewery can produce up to 2 million gallons per year, but there are different rules about ownership and ingredients.

So what's the right option for you?

My best advice is to drive around your town or city and make a mental note – or even better, a list – of the different types of breweries within your radius. I know I said that the craft beer community is a very friendly one, but the ones near you will be your direct competitors in business, after all – no harm scoping them out. Look at the demographics of your town. What are they looking for? Is there something that the other already existing breweries are not serving? Is your town slowly being gentrified? How about a new trend that hasn't reached your place yet? From there, you can slowly build or visualize your business plan, and you'll know what type of brewery will best sustain your business.

I'm going to throw out a guess that most of the readers of my book are planning to be an independent brewery. But before we delve even deeper, let's start with the basics or the definitions of the types of breweries you will encounter.

Types of Small Breweries

During surveys, beer drinkers – especially the craft beer lovers – say that they need to know if the beers are coming from an independent and small brewery first before buying or ordering. But as I said before, conglomerates are buying up independent brewers left and right for the past decade, hoping to join the bandwagon. So the Brewers Association came up with the **"Independent Craft Brewer"** seal to promote independent breweries and to rebel against these shrewd tactics.

To be considered **independent**, 25% of your brewery must not be owned or controlled by an alcohol industry member that is not considered as a craft brewer. A craft brewery is essentially an independent brewery. Compared to the larger conglomerate-run breweries or macro-breweries, independent craft breweries produce much smaller amounts of beer annually. A craft brewery will produce 6 million or fewer barrels of beer annually.

Breweries are then subdivided into different categories. Let's break them down according to the sizes of their production, from biggest to smallest.

The largest would be the **small independent craft brewers** who can produce 6 million barrels of beer per year – which is 3% in terms of market share. It might seem like a big amount, but it is relatively small when compared to the 200 million barrels produced each year in the US. It used to be required that their beer contained 50% malt, but the BA changed its definition back in December 2018—so you're free to follow your star and create what you like, to an extent. Whether you can sell your beer on site, and how much you can sell, depends on your state.

Next come the **microbreweries** who can produce

15,000 barrels a year or even less. Some microbreweries have tasting rooms or bars on-site, but 75% of their output must be sold through distribution or off-site.

Even smaller than microbreweries are the **nanobreweries** – also sometimes defined as taproom breweries because both brew such small quantities. The definition is quite vague on this one, but most people would say that nanobreweries must produce less than 2,000 barrels per year or brew 3 barrels of beer or even less in one batch.

A nanobrewery is an attractive prospect as it requires a lower capital, but since the work required to brew at least 3 barrels of beer is the same as when you want to brew 7 or 10 barrels, the margins will be thinner as well, resulting in lower profits. So a nanobrewery is only great when you want to start expanding from your homebrews to test the market or build a proof of concept before investing more money – it's not something that can rake in the cash.

There are 3 ways your brewery can manage its sales: direct sales, two-tier, and three-tier systems.

In direct sales, the brewery sells the beers directly to the consumer either in the taproom or in a restaurant on-site.

In the two-tier system, the brewery is the wholesaler and sells the beers to a retailer, who then sells them to the consumer.

In the three-tier system, the wholesaler and the brewery are separate. The brewery sells its beers to a wholesaler, who then looks for a retailer that can then sell it to the consumers.

What's a Brewpub?

Most people would categorize brewpubs and taproom breweries for the number of barrels they produce, but I would rather define them as brewery operation models for easier understanding when it comes to business plans.

A brewpub is a restaurant and a brewery combined. The beers are brewed on-site in smaller quantities as most of the beers are primarily just sold inside the restaurant – some even have exclusive brews only sold on-site to increase their desirability.

You could think of brewpubs as a middle ground or the gateway drug for people interested in knowing more about craft beer. Consumers who might not be that knowledgeable, or not that invested, can go to a brewpub with friends to eat, have a good time, and also sample some of the brews the brewpub has to offer. It's also not uncommon for brewpubs to feature "guest" beers on tap – beers from other independent breweries – along with other types of wine and liquor.

Commonly found in bustling downtown retail areas, a brewpub is a great business model if an existing restaurant wants to "upgrade" and jump into the brewery business. Brewpubs would also tend to curate their food offerings to complement the beers sold, therefore making the success of this model reliant on both the food served and the beers. Even if the main focus of the brewpub is the beers brewed on-site – which distinguishes them from a typical restaurant – owners must continuously strive to think of ways on how to entice customers to come in and enjoy themselves. This includes updating the menu, serving guest brews and other liquor, and creating a nice atmosphere for patrons to dine in.

More often than not, a brewpub would only usually serve locally inside the community. Depending on the state and the popularity and demand of its brews, it is sometimes legal for brewpubs to sell their beers off-site or to a retailer. In this case, the laws state that at least 25% of its beers must be sold on-site in the restaurant inside the brewery.

Taproom Breweries

A taproom brewery sells 25% or more of its beers on-site and sometimes through distributors and retailers off-site. But unlike a brewpub, it serves almost little to no food on-site; prepackaged cheese, pretzels, and cold cuts might sometimes be served, but for the most part, food preparation is not allowed. So a taproom is basically a place where you go to experience and taste the beer itself and buy exclusively brewed beers by the brewery, which you can savor inside or take home with you in growlers.

In terms of distribution, when compared to brewpubs, taprooms have fewer restrictions. In a taproom, you sell most of your beers off-site, but the on-site offerings inside the taproom can give you another stream of income. And since beer always goes well with food, recently, other hybrids of the taproom brewery are also popping up. A lot of taprooms now have partnered with food trucks and local restaurants, allowing their customers to bring over takeout. Some have even invited food trucks to permanently stay on location to serve their customers. Other entrepreneurs have also rented adjacent spaces beside their taprooms as their kitchens and have another business run them.

These taproom hybrids are a great choice if you want to be able to offer food on-site without worrying about restaurant operations. Some owners like it since they can concentrate solely on making beer, and because the food part is entirely separate from your brewery operation, if it does end up losing money, your brewery will be spared.

Farm Breweries

Farm breweries got their start from farmers who used to brew low ABV beer for their workers. These are quite different from the other models on this list because, like farms, they receive agricultural benefits and don't require a permit or a liquor license from the government to serve beer on-site – just the farm brewing license will do.

Crops raised in these farms are usually hops, barley, rye, corn, and wheat as farm breweries are required by law to grow ingredients used for brewing on the farm itself – the percentage of ingredients required to be grown in the farms vary depending on state laws. Also, depending on the legalities of each state, farm breweries can sell their brews off-site to various distributors and retailers.

The Basics of Beer Making

Repeat after me: water, malt, hops, and yeast. These are the all-important ingredients in beer making. Your business will largely depend on the quality of beer you're brewing.

You can't start a brewery without knowing how to brew beer (though technically you can – if you're good at crunching numbers and you already have startup capital, you can always find or hire a master brewer, but it will be a totally different experience). You can even partner up with a friend who already brews his own beers – maybe that dormmate of yours who sold his homebrews to all those college kids.

But enough rambling – here, I would like to point out that this book will not teach you all the different ways to brew beer because I'd like to believe that you already know how to brew your own and probably already have a nice setup at home. But for those of you who picked this book up on a whim, worry not – I got you covered with the basics.

Easy Home Brewing

However, if you've never made beer before, I suggest starting with a home brewing kit. It's everything you need for brewing up a small batch in a single box. No need to buy sacks of hops, malt, and yeast that you might not use again. I'm writing this during the 2020 pandemic, and everyone's going crazy – as a result, there are loads of home DIYs popping up everywhere. Just typing in "home beer brewing kit" will give you loads of options on Amazon. Even better, your local brewery or taproom might have a kit they'll sell you.

So, there are two types of home brewing. If you look through Amazon, you'll see kits marked as "all-grain" or "extract." If you don't already know, beer uses sugar extracted from malted grains. So if it says "all grains," it means you, as the brewer, will extract the sugar from the partially germinated grains yourself. However, when the kit you have found says "extract," it just means that the sugars from the grains have already been extracted for you. It's one less step. The latter (extract) is perfect for people just starting to experiment with home brewing. The steps are simpler as the extraction of the sugars has already been done, albeit partially, and you also won't need a lot of beer equipment. As for the taste, there won't be any difference between the two.

Here, we'll be strictly talking about extract brewing since it's the easier of the two and, as I said above, perfect for beginners. For those of you who already have home brewing setups at home, feel free to go on to the next chapter.

First, let's talk about the four basic ingredients:

Water makes up 90% of your beer, so this is very

important. You want to avoid water that has an odor, i.e., chlorine. It has to be clean and have moderate alkalinity and hardness, but tap water is also fine most of the time.

Malt and grains. In beer making, malt refers to the different types of malted grains – usually barley – that are partially germinated and dried. The grains are soaked in water until they begin to sprout. This germination process converts the grain's starch and protein into sugars and acids. Once they sprout, the grains are dried, creating malted grains. Beer brewers then crush the malted grains and soak them in water to release the sugars and make "wort" – unfermented beer – which is then boiled and fermented with the other ingredients to produce beer.

When using malt extracts, extracting the sugar has already been done for you, making it easier for brewers to make beer. These extracts are sold in the market in dry (DME) and liquid (LME) forms.

Some brewers also like to add "specialty grains," even if they are using malt extracts. These grains will lend added flavor, aroma, and body to the beer.

Hops. These are small green flowers from the plant *Humulus lupulus*. The alpha acids in them are responsible for that signature bitterness of beers – the higher the percentage of the acid, the more bitter your brew will become. The percentage of the acid will vary depending on a lot of different factors, like the region from where your hops originated, the variety, or even the year it was harvested. To achieve bitterness from the hops, they need to be boiled for about an hour, called "bittering."

On the other hand, in "dry-hopping," aromatic or finishing hops are also used to add flavor to your beer at the finishing stage. The finishing hops won't impart bitterness to your beer but only add aroma and fragrance because they'll only be added at the last few minutes of the boil.

Yeast comes in liquid and dry form and is used to ferment the wort. It converts the sugars extracted from the malt to produce CO_2 and alcohol. "Brewers make wort. Yeast makes beer." Without yeast, you'll have no beer.

So if you're planning to do this seriously, make it a habit to keep a record of your brewing recipes. Keep the packages of your hops so you can keep track of the acid percentage easily- it will help you improve your beers in the long run.

Okay, so let's take a crack at making your first batch of home-brewed beer. If you don't already have a beer brewing kit, here are the ingredients you'll need, as well as equipment, and step-by-step instructions.

Beer Making, Step-by-Step

You will need:

Your choice of specialty grains (1 lb)

Grain bag

Yeast

Malt extract

Hops (bittering and finishing)

Beer kettle or a large stockpot

Funnel (optional)

Stir spoon

Auto-siphon

Sanitizer (a sodium percarbonate cleaner)

Fermenter + Airlock

Cooking thermometer

First, you'll need to sanitize everything. There are cleaners available for this purpose on the market, like the sodium percarbonate cleaner PBW. When your beer is fermenting, you don't want any other contaminants in there or it could ruin the beer.

Let's start with one pound of grains. First, your grain needs to be crushed – gently, not pulverized. You want to just crack open each husk and break the kernel into about three pieces, so the water can pass through. You can do the crushing at home if you have a mill handy, or you can ask your brewer if they can kindly crush it for you.

To steep your grain: Place your grains in a grain bag. In a steel pot, bring 2 gallons of water to about 160 degrees. Lower the filled grain bag gently into the pot, and let it steep for about 20-25 minutes. Afterward, drain your grain bag while being careful not to squeeze it. Just let it drip into the pot.

Let the mixture come to a rolling boil, then take it off the heat. You can now add your malt extracts. Stir until all the malt has been dissolved and bring it back up to a rolling boil. You can add the hops in along with the malt extract, or you can choose to slowly add them in intervals as the mixture is boiling. This is your wort, and let it boil for 1 hour. This will release the bitterness from the hops. You can add aromatic or finishing hops into your boiling wort in the last 5 minutes of your boil. Hops added in the last 5 minutes will not add any bitterness to your beer but only give it added flavor and aroma.

Cool the wort as quickly as possible. If you're a beginner, you can use an ice bath – just let your pot sit in a bucket filled with ice water. Brewers use a wort chiller.

Make sure anything your wort touches after this is completely clean. Transfer the cooled-down wort to your fermenter and add cold water according to your recipe. Most recipes for home brewing will tell you to add water until you reach 5 gallons.

Shake your fermenter for a bit; your wort needs to be aerated so the yeast can start working. Then add your yeast or, as we say, "pitch the yeast." I suggest you use dry yeast first if you're a beginner. Your wort should be around 78°F before putting the yeast in, or you can always refer to the instructions that came with your yeast.

Seal up the fermenter and place the airlock. Store the fermenter in a cool, dry place and let the yeast do its magic for 1 to 2 weeks. Some brewers add a second fermentation for a clearer beer with fewer sediments.

Now it's time to bottle it! Make sure your bottles are sanitized (not just washed). Siphon the finished beer into the bottling bucket, careful to leave any sediments in the fermenter. This is the stage where you want to add any bottling additives your recipe calls for, like priming sugar. Store in your fridge. That's it! You've just made beer.

Getting Down to Business

Here's the question that's probably in your mind right now: Is 2021 realistically the best time to start a brewery business?

Sure, the craft beer industry has been booming for years now, with a growth of 3 to 4% annually, but the pandemic brought everything to a screeching halt. Now, the world is emerging from the chaos like a bedraggled survivor from a devastating earthquake. The world has been talking about a new kind of normal since last year, but will it still be applicable after the pandemic? Or will the world go back to the way it was before the pandemic? Did our demographic's taste and preferences change after this ordeal?

A lot of industries struggled during the last year, especially everyone in the food and beverage industry. We've seen closings everywhere, and a few businesses have had to take loans and cut back on their workforce in order to keep the business going. A few very quick-thinking breweries started to do deliveries and switched to online platforms. Since a lot of craft breweries are anchored to the local community, some of us managed to survive like this. We are holding on because beer is beer – I'd like to believe it's already an essential part of our lives, especially here in America.

So is now a good time to start a brewery? Realistically speaking, when you start planning for a brewery business in 2021, your brewery business will probably be taking baby steps by late 2022. Yes, that late. That's because you will have a lot of things to consider before your brewery can take off; plus, the legal part and the licenses could take a long time.

Our Story: Starting Out

Pops and I, as former admen, have had the pleasure to work with several breweries, big and small. We've helped them build their brands and capture the market, and given our family's affinity for beer, we've also worked as a team providing design consultancy services to small local breweries in our town. Starting our own brewery sort of had been out on the table for years and years before my dad passed away – we've just never truly acted upon it. It's always there – we'd already toyed with our logo and branding and even reached the point of scouting for a location.

It never came to fruition. Maybe back then, it was just a nice dream for us, but deep inside, I think I knew why we didn't act on it – we were afraid of it failing. If it's just a dream and you don't act on it, it will never have the chance to fail. But we figured, after he died, to honor him and his love for beer, we'd start a brewery in his name – to finally accomplish the dream we've had since I was still in university.

He found me brewing my own in the garage way back

when I was in high school. It didn't taste good. In fact, it sucked. But my friends and I were underage, and it got us drunk, so no one was complaining. Surprisingly, when my dad found out, he wasn't angry but actually supported my hobby. Together, we brewed our own beers, slowly building what we fondly called our "garage brewery." When I got older, we still occasionally brewed every so often, but we just didn't have enough time for it anymore. We were both so consumed with work and other things in life, but whenever I came back home, I'd always take him to pub runs. We'd talk for hours about work, about design, about beers. We'd go to a brewpub or a taproom, and we'd talk extensively on how we'd do it if we had our own.

When he left this world, my wife, in an effort to console me, brought the idea of a brewery back up. Our family is young – we were just starting out, and we wanted to be there for our children when they were growing up. We felt that working for an agency full time would rob us of time with our kids. My wife and I are both workaholics – we couldn't leave a project alone if we were not satisfied. We also didn't want our children to grow up with their parents seldomly home. In short, we didn't want our careers to be our entire lives.

So starting our own business seemed like a great prospect, and if it was successful, at the end of our years, we can proudly pass it on to our children – provided they also like beer. We talked to my mom about it, and she fully supported the idea. And we finally, after decades, got the ball rolling.

When we first started, we thought we knew everything about building our own business. We helped companies with their marketing and branding. How hard could it be? Suffice it to say that we underestimated the task. Being an entrepreneur needs a whole new different skill set. Heck, I studied arts because I was bad at math. I figured starting a business would just require a few simple calculations that could be done with a calculator. But boy, oh boy, was I ever wrong.

A startup brewery is not all about just brewing good beers. There's lots of competition out there, and in reality, there will always be people who make good or even better beers. Planning is a very big part of your beer journey.

As a future business owner, you need to be on top of a lot of things. It's not just your beer recipe and finances that you need to be worried about. – you also need to keep track of the regulations and laws of your state, the construction of your brewery, your equipment, your deliveries, etc.

You also need to have a pulse on what is going on in the market and in your demographic. This is so you can adjust or tweak your plan accordingly. Throw your pride and your stubbornness out of the window. Sure, your first plan may seem great at first, but as you steadily work on it and start to figure things out, you will find that what you initially had in your head might not work at all. Building a good business plan needs a lot of research, foresight, and understanding of the market.

It's a lot of work – trust me. But for this book, I sat down with my wife and wrote down what we think will help you a lot.

The Business Plan

Let's start with the thing most people put off if they can: the business plan. There's no other way around it – you need to formulate your business plan. Did you know that having a business plan makes sure that your business would have a 30% more chance at success instead of just winging it and going with the flow? You'll need to be flexible and adaptable to change; also, having a business plan will help you a lot when you want to raise your startup capital. When you want to apply for a loan, the bank or your potential investor will assume that you have one and will ask for it.

A great business plan can work as your business resume. It can attract potential investors, but it can also throw them off. It should also be updated as frequently as possible as you start to take steady steps towards your brewery. To start with, make sure to include an Executive Summary that is not longer than a page. Here, you'll need to summarize the overarching points of your business.

Include a business overview where you can highlight the basic information about your business, such as your address and contact details as well as your brewery's name.

In the business description, write down what you envision your brewery will be like. This is your business' vision mission that you will stick to as you grow. Also, include your brewery's concept and your proposed location.

Market and consumer analysis will tell your future investors about how well you know your demographic or market and the industry you are planning to break into. This is where your graph-making skills from your office job can come in handy. Detail what you know about your target market about how they will be likely to spend their cash in that particular location you proposed.

Also, report about the past and current trends of the brewery industry as well as the forecasts in the coming years. Make sure to include how everything relates to the demand of breweries that can make starting a brewery entirely feasible from a business standpoint. Don't just write that you love beer – basically, this is where you prove that if you open a brewery on this particular site or city and serve this particular market, it will do well and not go straight to bankruptcy after a few months.

In competitor analysis, you break down all the breweries near you and analyze how and why they work or don't and how you can come in and have a fighting chance to survive – or better yet, win. Keep in mind that you'll have indirect as well as direct competition too, so list down not only breweries if you're planning on taking on a retail space. If you are planning a brewpub, then include the dining options near you and why consumers will choose you.

You will also need to include your marketing strategy. Understand your own brewery's SWOT (strength, weakness, opportunities, and threats) and how you plan to attract consumers. Write down your proposed position in the market. Detail how you plan to price your menu and at least have a year's plan of how you'll be promoting your brewery.

The next section will be the operations. In this section, you need to outline how your brewery will operate on a day-to-day basis. This will include information about how you plan to staff your brewery, what suppliers you plan to use, as well as your business insurance and licensing requirements.

Lastly, the financials – in here, detail your brewery's

financial forecasts. This includes revenue, expenses, and operation costs. A good financial forecast will help you a lot if you plan on getting a loan or are trying to attract investors. Investors and banks invest for their financial growth, so prove to them that your business will make a profit and not just break even.

Market Research and Consumer Analysis

The first thing on your agenda is to conduct extensive research. Research your market A LOT. Don't just believe in taproom hearsays. Walk around town; check out all the breweries within your city. Don't just blindly believe it when that old dude in your favorite pub says that the vacant lot in the 2nd street is a perfect place for your brewery. The same is true with random comments from strangers online and offline. If a handful of students from the local college tells you that they love your beer, it doesn't mean that they are your demographic. In this vein, find out more about your demographic too.

Craft beer surged in popularity due to the changing tastes of the demographic. A large percentage of our demographic for years now have been millennials, but now that the Gen-Z's are coming of age, the tastes for craft beer are bound to change again. It's not going to be a huge shift, but more like subtle shifts in preferences and consumer behavior. According to various data, the younger generation also prefers local and small, so there are no worries about craft beer being pushed out of business.

But the new generation will care more about what you do than what you are. For example, they won't just support a local business just because they're local. They will want to know what you are doing as a business and how you are contributing to the community. Research shows that this generation's buying preferences will be deeply rooted in ethics, on how you do as an individual or as a business, so your business must not only be local but morally and ethically conscious as well.

Out of all the generations, they will be the most connected, which is why they'll have the means and skill to find out what they want to know about your business quickly. Besides this, the younger crowd will also be drinking less, but at the same time, they want quality drinks too. They won't just go out for a night in town for drinks and get dead drunk when morning comes – hence the emergence of beers with lower ABV. Some even have 0% alcohol beer on tap.

When they go out for a night of fun in the city, they also want activities and experiences to go with it. That's why themed restaurants and cafes are popping up all over the world. From gamer-themed restaurants to art and owl cafes, the brewpubs and taprooms are joining the bandwagon too.

So, don't just blindly open a brewery when your friends

encourage you to. Encouragement and support from friends and family are good for obvious reasons, but they won't know anything about your market. Your circle of friends in your town might love beer, but that will be a very small percentage of your town's population that you're sure will drink your craft beer. What about the rest of the folks in your town? Will they love craft beer as well? What if the demographic in your town is filled with boomers who love Budweiser's better? Your business can't make a profit or even meet margins if you'll only be counting on a few customers every day to drink a bottle or two.

Figuring out your demographic or market is the first step for your brewery. From here, you can have a clearer vision of what kind of business model you want to stick with. In the first chapter, I briefly touched upon niche breweries. I have also advised you to walk around your city or town to get a feel of what your intended market wants or what the gaps you can fill up could be.

The basic models of a brewery, as I've discussed earlier, are brewpubs, taprooms, and micro or nano breweries. Recently, contract brewing companies have also started popping up. These are companies where a business can hire you, the brewer, to make the beers for them and will also be responsible for the beer's marketing and distribution.

Now, do you have enough belief in your brewing skills that you want a microbrewery so your beers can be sold all over the States and can compete in shelf spaces and SKUs? Or maybe you know someone who cooks the best dishes that pair well with your beers so you can open a brewpub? Or maybe you want to feel like a master brewer in a small town and open a taproom?

If you think only in terms of brewpubs and taprooms, think again – hybrids are now all over the place. You'll likely find the most innovative ones in cities or gentrified townships. They understand their market, and use innovation and creativity to appeal to their chosen niches.

Niche Markets

A lot of breweries have gone on to become successful through said innovation. There's one called "Signature Brew" in the UK that collaborates with renowned artists to produce beers. The brewery also has a taproom that can host live performances, effectively capturing the niche for music lovers out there who want to enjoy a night with a good quality beer in hand while they bang their heads to the drums and riffs of rock bands.

Some microbreweries decided to cater to the ethically conscious consumers making vegan beer, while some brewpubs have gone on to expand, managing to cater to both older and younger demographics by having two floors. The above floor has more sitting room and caters to the older market for them to drink and savor their beer in relative peace, while the floor below where various games are found are frequented by the younger crowd.

If you're still not sure where your future brewery will stand in the market, this is where a nanobrewery might come in handy. A nanobrewery is small enough that you don't need a lot of capital to get started. If you already have a decent home brewing setup in your house that can produce a few barrels of beer, you can test your recipe out in the market by joining fairs and farmer's markets.

Location

You also need to scout for the perfect location for your brewery – a good location can make or break it.

First, your vision for your brewery should already be clear in your head, so you'll know how much space you need from the very start. Ask yourself and your partners what you want the space to do for you. There are lots of things to consider: large storage space for your products, serving areas, dining areas, your main brewing area, parking spaces, loading and unloading area for shipments and deliveries, etc.

Next, you should familiarize yourself with the various laws surrounding breweries – and there's a lot of laws and licenses you need to read up on if you want to start on this journey as the brewery industry is one of the most regulated in this country. You'd also want to find a location that can cater to most if not all of your needs. Walk around and list down spots that will have no problem attracting your potential market. Scout the area for a place where you can stand out and innovate at the same time. For example, if your intended market is younger and you are living near a university town, it will make sense to scout for locations there.

Zoning is another thing to consider as cities and states have laws where they basically dictate what kind of industry you can build in a particular area. Before the craft beer boom, breweries could only be set in locations zoned for manufacturing. Thankfully, government agencies changed the zoning requirements a few years back, allowing breweries to place themselves smack dab in the center of commercial spaces.

Zoning laws vary from state to state. Approval of your brewery's potential site relies on many factors. These include adequate parking and the impact on local traffic. Consider your deliveries and if you want to distribute regionally. You will also need to meet requirements for proper wastewater discharge and dimensions.

As such, zoning laws are sometimes tricky to navigate. It's recommended that you call up your local planning department or a permitting specialist for help. You can also opt to hire a law firm or a lawyer who specializes in zoning bylaws.

Aside from attracting customers, your location should at the same time have good accessibility for shipping and deliveries, either for distribution or bringing in supplies. It should also have the right size and facilities. The size should fit what you want to do. Allocate smartly and make sure you have ample space for the business model and brewing equipment you will be using.

Will you be doing a brewpub? Then you would need to have a separate space for your brewery, a specialized kitchen, and your main dining area. A taproom might not need such a big dining area, but if you're planning to lease out an adjacent kitchen space or let a food truck be a permanent fixture for your taproom, then it would be smart to plan for a bigger space.

A lot of owners that I've talked to over the years have similar regrets 2 to 3 years into the business. They all wish that they could have gone for a location that had room for further expansion. I understand that as a beginner, you would want to keep everything within or lower in the budget, but seriously, consider taking up space 2 to 3 times bigger than you originally intended. Sure, you can save money at the start with a smaller location, but as your business expands naturally over the course of a few years, your space will not have any room for your future plans. You'd then have no choice but to move to a bigger place, thereby increasing your cost.

Still, remember to keep your flights of fancy in check. Don't be too over ambitious and decide to rent or lease space so big you end up not using most of it and lose more money than you originally wanted to save. The key here is to understand your business potential and your plans for the future. If you want to stick to the image of a medium-sized taproom and will only be serving your beers locally, then you obviously wouldn't want a huge space that looks like it could be a microbrewery that has the capacity to brew beers to be distributed across the region. Also, check what facilities are already in place in the location. I know someone who's lucky enough to lease a space that used to be a small winery. A lot of the things he needed were already in place, and he ended up saving tons construction-wise.

Speaking of construction, when picking out the right spaces, it's also best if you have an architect you can call to help you figure things out. Ask around, and you might find architects that are well-versed in designing brewery spaces. If they work locally, they would know a lot about the state requirements too, so that will save you more time. That vacant spot that you kind of like but think is too small might actually work if you consult an architect beforehand. Besides, an ingeniously designed space, aside from looking spectacularly good, will not only save you money but also attract visitors.

Take a look at Bluejacket's "The Arsenal," which is housed in a soaring warehouse that used to store munitions in DC's old navy shipyard. The brewery equipment is arranged in a series of mezzanines and platforms that overlook the main dining space. It's the perfect example of design meeting function.

Equipment

Now, if you're a beer-lover like us who used to have setups at home, you probably already know a thing or two about beer equipment. There are plenty of options in the market, and choosing the right equipment will save you from headaches in the long run.

The right equipment for your brewery will depend on a few factors, like your potential space, what kind of beer you want to make, your brewing process, as well as how many barrels you will be producing. You need to be clear on what kind of beer you want coming out of your tap. If you don't want to scrimp on quality and insist on doing it the artisanal way (letting the beer ferment for twice as long), you will be needing more space for that in order to have beer constantly on tap for your consumers.

The location and your equipment will go hand-in-hand for the most part, and you will be spending the largest chunk of your budget on both. For example, a new seven-barrel system can cost you roughly $130,000- $175,000, so it's best to think this through very carefully. Talk to equipment vendors that specialize in the type of beer you plan to make. Shop around to compare prices and technology. It can also help if you talk to other breweries and take brewery tours. Familiarize yourself with how different breweries do their business, how they brew, where they brew, what their setup is, and how it's working for them.

If you're thinking of purchasing used equipment to save money, I'll tell you right off the bat that it's not a very good idea. Used brewery equipment is almost as expensive as new. You also won't have a warranty in case something happens. Besides, your brewery equipment will serve you for the next several years, and upgrading is also expensive. My suggestion is to figure out how you plan to brew and how you really see your business going for a year or two.

Overspending is easy, and you can get carried away with all the choices. Buying the correct size for your brewery will be a balancing act. Starting small will incur more expenses in the future when you suddenly can't keep up with the demand. The higher cost of buying smaller batches of ingredients will also trickle down to your pricing, making your brews more expensive. But starting bigger will also put a strain on your budget, not to mention that a mistake in brewing on a larger scale will be very costly for a startup. Spending a huge chunk of your money, or worse, your investor's money, on larger equipment with any established demand will cripple you.

This is why I told you to study your market. If you feel like you will outgrow a small setup in just half a year into your operations, then it's best to invest in something with a larger capacity.

It's true that you need to start with a bigger location that has room for expansion in the coming years, but the same does not apply to your brewery equipment. A smart thing to do is to start with a smaller brewery with enough room for a dedicated boil kettle or a whirlpool in the future. Then, you can go bigger with your fermenter tanks – around double the size of your brewhouse should be enough. These tanks can be filled halfway or all the way to capacity depending on your brewery's actual demand.

To best gauge how big your brewery should be, try to calculate your annual brewing capacity. Your annual capacity is your daily fermenting volume multiplied by your turns per year.

To calculate the daily fermenting volume, you need to find out your intended number of vessels multiplied by the vessels' volume.

To calculate for turns per year, you need to divide the number of brew days you'll have in a year by the number of days your beer takes to ferment on average. If your planned brewery calls for a lot of rotating beers on tap at any given time, you can think about acquiring the same ratio of rite and fermenting tanks.

Finances and Start-up Costs

Fairly large investment capital is going to be needed for your brewery. Yes, you could try running a nano brewery on a piece of land you own – provided your state and zoning laws allow it. But it will undoubtedly be one costly project. Unlike other startups, aside from the basic overhead and infrastructural costs needed by any other business, a brewery will need a lot of equipment and a larger location as well.

And as in every startup, your brewery will have its own startup expense. These are what we usually call upfront costs that you'll be meeting before you can even start your brewery and earn revenue.

Upfront costs – one time expenses

Applicable licenses, permits, and bonds from federal and state offices

Down payment and deposit for your leased or rented location

Construction costs

Insurance

Branding and packaging costs

Start-up assets – long-term assets that your brewery will need to run

Brewery equipment

Bottling equipment – for when you plan to distribute your beers regionally or for export

Kitchen equipment – for when you want your brewery to serve food

Starting inventory

Monthly ongoing expenses

Beer ingredients and cleaning supplies

Salaries

Bills and taxes

Insurance premiums

Marketing and advertising costs

Rent

Loan payments

What to Consider with Financial Planning

Your brewing equipment would be one of the more costly things on your expenditure list, and it will depend on the size of your brewery. Some startups prefer to buy used equipment in hopes that they will save more, but I say invest in new brewing equipment.

As I've discussed above, your brewing equipment will serve you for several years if you plan right. The smallest capacity, a 1-barrel brewing system, will set you back $100,000 brand new, while a 30-barrel system will cost you $1,000,000 brand new. There will be cheaper equipment available in the market, but most will come from countries outside of the US where production cost is cheaper. The problem with this is you compromise quality, and it might be more costly to repair if something goes wrong, especially if there's no service available.

The construction you'll be needing before you start your business is also expensive. If you go with a bigger location right in the middle of the city, your rent will take up a huge portion of your monthly expenses. The landlord will also ask for the first month's rent in a security deposit when you go in to sign the lease. And when you've leased the building, you will need to alter a lot of things to make it fit for a brewery.

Since your brewery will be inspected if it complies with regulations set by the state and Federal law, you will also need to consider a lot of requirements like electrical, plumbing, drains, structural integrity, and ceiling height.

You shouldn't forget the flooring too. I have some acquaintances that had to tear out the whole concrete floor to change it to a good composite floor that can withstand temperature and impact shocks as well as the acid from the beer you pour out.

Depending on what building you use, if you need to do a lot of work before you can run with it, your construction costs will, of course, ramp up. It will be very expensive to convert a commercial space that used to be just a storehouse into a brewery. You'll basically be rebuilding the whole thing from the ground up, retaining just the skeleton and the facade. If it doesn't have water lines, drains, ventilation, etc., you're better off with another location if you are on a tight budget.

This is why you should talk to an architect or a contractor who specializes in breweries early in your plans. They will know how big the construction project will be and if there are any red flags in the space before you rent it out. As a general rule, your construction cost will be double your equipment cost.

The people you hire who will help you build your

project are also going to cost you a lot too, like designers, accountants, lawyers, architects, conductors, and consultants. There's just no other way around it. It would be better to get everything right on the first try than find out you're wrong when you're already operating. That might end up costing you a lot more.

Your business plan also shouldn't be set in stone. A brewery's main focus is beer, yes. But if the opportunity comes and you have a chance to increase revenue by focusing more on food, you must be ready to assess your plan again. If you see that your beer has a chance to get more popular in the international market, trying to export your products might be a good idea. In short, be ready to pivot your business where it needs to go in order to stand out and increase revenue.

It will also be good to have all of your equipment installed and operational before TBB approves your Brewer's Notice. You have to pay monthly expenses before you can even legally brew and sell beer, so you will need working capital too.

Working Capital

Running a brewery will not always be smooth sailing. There will be delays and unexpected snags that can drag on for months, much like how this pandemic dragged on for more than a year. Simply put, working capital is capital from your business that can be used in day-to-day operations while you're not earning anything yet. It is used to measure your business' financial health on a short-term basis and see if you have enough money to go around to meet your other financial liabilities—things like your employees' salaries, ingredients, supplies, etc.

To check if you have enough working capital to meet your other financial obligations, subtract your current liabilities from your current assets. Also, when you formulate your financial plan, anticipate your delays and make adjustments to accommodate even your worst-case scenarios. Make sure that your capital can handle these setbacks easily.

Try to aim for an April to May opening, as winter is off-season for breweries. By aiming for a spring opening just when the beer-drinking season starts, hopefully, you won't be using too much of your working capital, and your business can run smoothly.

If your beer recipes are your most cherished babies, then your ledger should be its twin. A lot of brewers don't know that they also need to focus on the numbers when running a business. You're a business owner now; your ledgers should be one of your most prized possessions too.

Keys to Healthy Finances

Good accounting tells you about the overall health of your business. Not only can it help you get out of trouble, but it can also help you plan your future moves, check if it's the right time to expand, earn more, etc. To keep track of your business's financial health, here are some points to remember:

> Within the first 6 to 12 months of your brewery's operation, you need to be able to earn even just a small profit or at least break even.

> To break even means that the money you earn during operation is just enough to cover the cost of

your day-to-day operations without dipping into your capital.

This is different from the payback period, which is the time it takes for your business to recover from all money you poured into it when you first started.

In short, the payback period is when you've earned back the capital investment, and now you're profiting. And after the first 12 months, at the lowest point, you should see your brewery at least breaking even quarterly. It means that the brewery can keep going.

Next, in the coming 12 to 18 months from the start of the operation, most breweries start profiting around 10% at the lowest, so yours should too.

If you opened to a resounding success, look around and check your capacity. Is your supply able to meet its demand? Or is your brewery struggling to meet it? Will you need to buy or upgrade your equipment?

Is your brewery's cash flow healthy? Cash flow pertains

to how much money is flowing in (sales, loans, investment returns, etc.) and out (bills, loan and tax payments, salaries, etc.). To calculate, it's net cash flow = cash received − cash spent.

You would want your net cash flow to be positive quarterly, if not monthly. This shouldn't be confused with profit. Your business can be profitable but still running out of cash because profits include everything—even items under your accounts receivable. Revenue on paper does not equate to cash. If you invoice your customer, but they haven't transferred the money to your account yet, that number is going to accounts receivable. Cash is the amount of money you currently have in your account, and it needs to be liquid; if you can't use it, it's not cash.

A positive cash flow means you are not struggling to pay your bills, your suppliers, or buying ingredients and supplies. If your cash flow is negative, and all your profits are in accounts receivable, you need to re-evaluate. Your negative cash flow is also your cash burn rate. Using that, figure out how many more months you can keep going if your cash flow is landing on negative monthly.

Try to keep your leverage – the ratio between your business's net worth and total liabilities – small.

It's a healthy habit to know how to do your accounting or at least know how to read your ledgers. If you really can't wrap your head around the numbers, you can hire an accountant to do the monthly or quarterly numbers-crunching for you. If you do end up doing it yourself, put together a cash flow and a sales forecast that you can monitor monthly.

To roughly estimate how much your full startup cost will be, calculate the monthly expenses or the cash that is going to flow out of your brewery in the first few months of your operation. Then estimate how many months before your brewery can break even – most breweries can reach the break-even point within the first 6 to 12 months. Take that number and add your upfront and startup assets. This will be – roughly – your entire startup cost.

Funding

Now let's talk about where you'll be getting your funding. Unless you're a trust fund baby, it will be hard for smaller startups to consolidate enough money by themselves to start a brewery. Remember, your investors will only invest if they feel like your brewery has the potential to earn profit. No one is just going to give their money to you just because you need it.

So, when looking at your business, it's also smart to look at it from the investor's perspective. Veteran investors know what to look for in a business before they invest. For a brewery, the first thing they need to know would be how good you are as a brewery plus your experience. A brewer that has won awards and has worked for an established brewery somewhere else for an extended period of time has a better chance of getting funding than when compared to a homebrewer who started in his garage 3 years ago. That's the sad truth. It's just like applying for a job. People with lesser experience also have a lesser chance of getting hired.

Another thing investors look at is your credit. A person with tons of debt in the bank will not get their loan approved, so make sure you have a good credit score. This will make you look like a responsible adult who is careful about your finances.

They will also look at how much money you already have in the pool. Access to contingency capital is also a good idea. A contingency capital will protect your business from failing by providing access to funds when a certain threshold or contingency is breached, i.e., natural disasters or needing another round of funding.

There are lots of ways to finance your business.

Let's start with your friends and family. Depending on your relationship with people around you, this might be easy – or not. Asking your friends and family and your networks to invest in your business is the most popular way startup breweries scrape for funding.

You can also opt for a home equity loan or use your retirement accounts. But do understand that tapping into your retirement funds is very risky. You also need to pay taxes and fees if you decide to. If you really want to, the IRS has "Rollover as Business Start-up" that will let you avoid penalties and other taxes.

You can also go for another recently popular mode: crowdfunding. Reward funding, like the ones from popular sites like Indiegogo and Kickstarter, will give your investors rewards for the small amount they invest. Equity crowdfunding, on the other hand, will give your investors a percentage of your company when they invest.

Angel funding is also an option. The investors are usually veterans in the industry and have a high net worth. If you can prove that your business model is unique and can give them a high return, they will invest. Another good thing about angel funding is that you can usually consult with them and ask for advice about your business.

I will reiterate – a brewery will require a large startup fund, and it can go for years until you finally make a profit. If you're planning to use this brewery to get rich fast, then you'll be better off with another business venture. As your demand increases and your supply can't catch up, you will be putting more and more money into it, whether to upgrade your equipment or expand to a bigger location.

This time, it's your love for beer and other factors that will make you stick to it. If you're nervous that it might not work out, just look at the number of breweries opening every day. It was estimated that there are 2 breweries opening every day in the US alone. Sure, there will come a time when the market will reach saturation and slow down, but that's still far into the future. For now, just try to get your funding.

Lager Laws

As I said earlier, the alcohol industry is one of the most regulated industries in the country, governed by both federal and state laws. That's why it is highly important that you familiarize yourself with the various laws and requirements needed in order to start your own brewery without any hiccups. At the federal level, the alcohol industry is under the TTB or the Alcohol and Tobacco Tax and Trade Bureau. Laws under the federal level can only inform you of the foundation because at the business level, it's the state law that will ultimately dictate how your business will be operating. You will need to meet requirements from several federal, state, and local authorities.

After the Prohibition era, the 21st Amendment passed in December 1933 and left the states to decide for themselves on how they would like to legalize alcohol. This ultimately led to the creation of the 3-tier system. The separation of the 3 bodies in the distribution and sales of alcohol was made to abolish the vertical monopolies that reigned during the early 20th century. Bars and saloons known as "tied houses" were "tied" to the brewers themselves. These monopolies drove down alcohol prices, got their patrons drunk, and are seen as a den filled with prostitution, gambling, and other vices. In the 3-tier system, the producers and brewers were entirely separate from the middle man or the distributors. The producers sold their beer to the middleman, who then sold it to the retailers.

The 3-tier system made it hard for the alcohol industry to be monopolized. The distributors or the small and independent middlemen were there to limit the power of the corporations up top. It was meant to ensure morality and promote diversity by checking and balancing the power of the corporate giants, but at the same time giving equal opportunity for startups to grow. It either prohibited or limited the way large producers could control or own the retailers.

And it worked fairly well until it didn't. During the last 30 years, we had 48 major brewers here in the United States merge into 2 corporate behemoths: Anheuser-Busch, InBev, and MillerCoors. Note that these are the two largest players in the United States alcohol industry. Also worth noting is that through recent acquisitions and mergers, the middle tier in most states is now mainly controlled by the "Big Two," namely, ABI and Miller Coors. This makes access to local markets harder, which then endangers the diversity and independence of the distributors and of craft beer itself. There are other small distributors out there, but their numbers are decreasing over time due to the countless mergers and acquisitions.

In an effort to cap this, the United States Department of Justice, as a condition to approving the SABMiller acquisition, limited the branch ownership of ABI to just 10% of its total beer volume in the United States.

But still, the current 3-tier system has allowed small independent businesses to be fairly successful while inside it. For example, beer distribution is an expensive endeavor. A small-time brewery would never have enough capital to afford to distribute their beers in a wider network and would have to settle with serving in a very limited area. By using the middle tier, a fledgling brewery can offer its beers to a larger market. Distributors, too, by handling many different brands, can afford to make logistics more efficient.

There are also a lot of local trade groups all over the country who are working hard to try to influence the policies and regulations surrounding our industry. As such, the policies and regulations can evolve over time and are always susceptible to change. And luckily, with the craft beer industry booming, a lot of state and federal laws did change to make the business environment more feasible and friendlier to business owners.

In fact, some state laws actually provide a lot more flexibility when it comes to brewery business models. In brewpubs, the producer and the retailer tier are allowed to merge together for a single business model. Some also allow breweries to have tasting rooms or restaurants on their premises. While other states even go as far as allowing small brewers to open their own retail shops. So, it's a good idea to know the people who are tasked to make these amendments and be constantly updated with what's happening in our industry.

And while change is good, not all compliance with the state and federal laws is easy. You need a lot of patience for these things as you start to navigate bureaucracy and red tape. There will be a lot of paperwork involved as well as filling and waiting to get approvals and permits.

Every state will also have its own specific requirements in regards to opening your brewery. But here's a simple guide on what you'll need to start with.

Legal Identity, Business Name, and Trademark

First, you need to figure out what kind of business structure you'd like for your business. The business structure you end up choosing will dictate how much taxes you will be paying, your personal liability, and your ability to raise money. You'll also need it before you can register your business and file or apply for various permits and licenses as dictated by the law. At this point, it will be very wise to consult or ask for advice from people that are experts in this field, like accountants, lawyers, and business consultants.

You'll have a few choices: LLC (Limited Liability Company), sole proprietorship, partnership, corporations, and cooperatives. But we'll only be talking about the first three structures that I find will suit most small brewery startups.

A sole proprietorship is the easiest to set up as it's the most basic of all business types that you can establish. In a sole proprietorship, you will be the sole business owner and will be held personally responsible for all the assets and liabilities of your business. Your personal assets will not be separated from your business assets and liabilities and will not be protected if anything happens to your business.

Banks will also be less than willing to approve your loan if you are in one. However, a sole proprietorship is a good choice for small businesses with low risks. A few business owners also find a sole proprietorship as a way to test their ideas before jumping into other business structures.

In a partnership, you can have two or more people own the business together. In a Limited partnership or LP, you have only one partner who can have unlimited liability; all the others would have limited liability and would also usually have limited control over the business too. In Limited Liability Partnerships or LLP, all the members have limited liabilities, protecting each from debts against the partnership. Partnerships can be a good choice for groups like law and architectural firms and businesses with multiple owners.

An LLC allows more than one person to own a business and is perfect for businesses that have medium to high-risk profiles. It will also give your brewery better protection as it will give you all the limited liability features you would normally find in corporations the benefits of a partnership. In an LLC, your personal assets will be separated and protected from your business assets and liabilities. You will not be held personally accountable when your business fails. The tax rate is also lower than you would pay for in a corporation. However, you will still be considered as self-employed, and members must pay tax contributions to Social Security and Medicare.

To create a legal identity for your brewery, you would need an official business name that you can trademark. Think carefully and think it through. This name can't be changed easily once you've submitted it. It should also be uniquely yours and cannot be trademarked by anyone else before you. Check with the databases in the United States Patent and Trademark offices. A name too similar to an already existing company will not only create confusion between your businesses but also give you a hard time in the future during expansion plans. Also, try to make your trade name and your business' legal name the same. In some states, you cannot operate your business if both names are different.

It's not only the brewery name that you should be filing trademarks for. Your logos and names of your beers should also be trademarked – you can trademark the names of your beers 36 months in advance before it drops. If you already have a list handy, you can submit them all in one go to reduce the hassle.

Brewer's Notice in the TTB

Under federal law, you will need to submit a "Brewer's Notice" to the Alcohol and Tobacco Tax and Trade Bureau (aka, the TTB) before you can begin operations. The TTB is under the United States Treasury and is in charge of regulating and collecting the taxes on various goods, including alcohol in the US.

Out of all the permits you will be applying for, this will take the longest time to process. If you're unlucky, it might take up to a year, so be sure to set aside ample time and do this in advance. This will also require a lot of paperwork; plus, you should already have proof that you have investors or funding and a copy of your lease, among other things. The TTB will also ask you to submit various information like your packaging, labels, and your brewery's environmental impact, as well as a "brewer's bond," which we'll be discussing below.

Brewer's Bond

Your brewery will also need to pay a federal excise tax for the beers you're planning to sell. A brewer's bond will simply guarantee that you'll be paying your taxes regularly. TTB also won't approve your "Brewer's Notice" if you don't have a bond.

A brewer's bond will have two forms: a surety bond and a collateral bond. A surety bond is backed by a surety company that will charge you an annual fee for guaranteeing the payment for your excise tax liability – their annual fees can range from 1% to 15%. A collateral bond, on the other hand, is paid by the business owner either by money order or by check. If your brewery's tax liability is smaller than $5,000, you can take the collateral bond.

The amount of your bond will depend on whether you plan to file excise tax returns semi-annually or quarterly. If you plan to pay your taxes quarterly, your excise tax for the whole year should be below $50,000, and your bond should be 29% of your tax. If your excise tax goes above $50,000, you'll have to pay them semi-monthly, and your bond should be 10% of it.

To calculate the amount of your bond, you will need to first figure out the excise tax you'll be paying in one calendar year. So, if your brewery has an annual production yield of just up to 60,000 barrels per year, then your excise tax should be $3.50 per barrel. It's $18 per barrel if your annual yield is above 60,000 but below 2,000,000 barrels.

You then multiply your excise tax by either .29 (if you are paying monthly) or .10 (if you're paying quarterly.

So, for example, if you'll be paying semi-monthly and you produce 50,000 barrels in a year, the amounts should be:

    Excise tax = 175,000

    Bond= 17,500

The bond expires after 4 years, so you will need to repeat your calculations again and reapply. Aside from the brewer's bond, you might also be needing a "local brewer's bond" if your state requires it.

Other Licenses

"Brewer's Notice" is under federal law, but you will be needing an alcoholic beverage permit from the appropriate offices in your state too.

There will be lots of licenses available, so you need to decide what kind you will need. For example, the manufacturer, retailer, and wholesaler licenses are totally different, and whatever license you get will depend upon your business and how you plan to operate it. The amount of beer you plan to produce annually will also determine what kind of license you need. It can also affect your licensing fee.

Here's a few common examples of brewery and food licenses that your state might have:

Restaurant liquor and all liquor license

This license will allow your brewery to serve not only

beer and wine but other alcohols and spirits too. However, some states might limit the percentage of revenue that will be coming from your alcohol sales

Beer and wine liquor license

This license will only allow you to sell beer and wine

Tavern license

For when your sales from alcohol alone are more than 50% of your whole revenue; this license is great for brewpubs that sell food alongside their beers

Server license

For states like Indiana and New Mexico, servers dealing with alcohol are required to have their own permits

When applying for the state licenses, it's also best if you have already prepared the proper documents about your brewery's location and your financial documents, as these are prerequisites in every state.

Did you take bank loans, or do you have investors? The financial documents you will be submitting must clearly state how you will be financing your brewery, so include a "statement of funding sources." Make sure that you are complying with federal and state laws, especially when dealing with your finances.

Here's a list of what you might need to submit to your state:

Liquor license application

Documentation about your brewery's location

Most states will require you to either be in the process of renting, owning, or leasing the property you will be using or are done with all of it. When your application is finally being reviewed, your brewery's location will be inspected to see if it complies with all the state and federal requirements.

Your financial documentation and statement of funding

Your brewery's floor plans

Make sure this complies with your state regulation depending on your business model.

Your "Brewer's Bond"

BONUS: food services requirements if you're planning on serving food

Insurance

As with any other business venture, you also need insurance for your brewery. There's plenty of things that can go wrong with your brewery when it's finally under operation, like problems with your drains and sewers, breakdown of your chiller, your employees spraining themselves from lifting heavy objects, and so on. Keep in mind that worker's compensation is mandatory if you have a few employees on your payroll. You'll need employment practices liability insurance or EPL. You will also need casualty property and liability insurance. All three will be needed if you want to ask a bank for a loan.

Basically, anything that can cause lost revenue for your brewery can be covered by extensive insurance coverage, so make sure your brewery is adequately insured to keep the costs lower.

In the end, don't even try to handle all of the legalities by yourself if you have never had any experience dealing with businesses and legal things before. It is highly recommended that you hire a trusted business consultant or a lawyer that specializes in breweries or wineries to help you navigate through all these. The legal matters in your business shouldn't be just tossed to the side. It's very important, and you don't want anything to go wrong with it.

Sell, Sell, Sell: Branding

Branding and Logos

The craft beer market is crowded. There are already lots of award-winning breweries that have been in the game since the start of the craft beer boom. But there's a way to make sure you stand out, and that's with your branding and marketing strategy. The beer you serve is your brewery's soul, while your branding is its visible outer shell – how your consumers see your business. Your marketing strategy is how you dress. Everything you used to percent your brewery should match up or complement each other.

Craft breweries all across the country come in different shapes and sizes, and smartly using your branding can make you stand out in a sea of brewers – that, and a very, very good marketing plan, both of which go hand-in-hand. Working in an agency, I've had the pleasure to launch breweries big and small, among other things. It's such a thrill to see startups going head-to-head with industry bigshots in SKUs war and winning. And it's such fun to think of ways on how to make the product more appealing to the market.

To start it all off, you need to have branding. But to have good branding, you need to know your target market first. You can either do this yourself and hire a third-party market research agency to do it for you. It doesn't matter whether you plan to have a brewpub or a microbrewery that distributes regionally or if you go worldwide – I mean, why not? Sky's the limit! Instead of going through trial and error, good market research can save you a lot of time and money from the get-go. And if you are planning to distribute to retailers, I suggest you contact a good market research agency.

Good market research will help you figure out if your business has a space within your target market's needs and wants. It will show you how and where you should stand so you can appeal to your market. And in tandem with a good marketing strategy, you can play up your strengths, opportunities, and even your weaknesses to your advantage, making it key to your success, especially if you are planning to distribute regionally.

Did you know that bigger brands actually test their beers first within a smaller group of their target market to know if their beers will be well-liked? I know that we as brewers take pride in our own recipes and beers, but we mustn't be afraid of listening to constructive criticisms. If your market says they don't like the taste of your beer, then either shift your focus to another group or change your recipe altogether. Just because you love your beer or your friends and a few select people like it doesn't mean that your whole target market will like your beer.

But! If you've managed to build a very successful brand — let's say you already have a name for yourself and even won beer competitions and such – and you come up with a beer that is not that good, sometimes, the taste won't matter anymore. Now, we brewers take pride in how we brew our beer. We are artisans! But I'm talking about the market of casual drinkers you've already reached that don't care much about taste. For instance, if you've exported your product to another country with exclusive rights in a posh club, then you will rake in the sales just because your name or brand is attached to it. Why do you think brands pay millions of dollars for endorsers? It's the same thing.

Humans are visual creatures, and memory and taste are very finicky. Sure, you can make a name for yourself with really good beer, but how good will it be compared to all the other award-winning beers in the craft beer market right now? How will you compete?

An example of a brand that has good branding and coupled with a great relationship with its consumers is the soda giant Coca-Cola. Between Coke and Pepsi, Coca-Cola is more popular – they've built such a good brand that when people think cola, they think Coke a large percent of the time. To combat this, Pepsi's marketing team conducted a taste test – back then, they were still newcomers to the scene – and Pepsi actually won. Still, they failed to cement their status because people tend to choose Coke because it's Coke – not because of its taste but because of the brand relationship they have built over the years with their consumers.

Likewise, you need your business to be the first thing that comes to your target market's mind when they want to go enjoy beers. This is the goal of almost all brands: to make their product a part of their consumers' lives. This is called brand loyalty. Your consumers will pick your brand out of everything in the market because, in their eyes, your product either serves them the best or is the best.

Brand loyalty ensures that you will have repeat and loyal customers. And to build it, you need to see how your intended target market behaves around your indirect and direct competitors. Good branding's role is to make you more relatable and memorable to your target market, but before you can build on your image, you need to make one first.

So at the start of your planning stage, talk to your designer or, if you're feeling fancy, your design agency. It's better to build a good relationship with the designer doing your logo and your branding so you can easily convey what you want your brand to look and feel like. Let them know your visions and the goal for the future of the business. You have a mood board? Pegs on how you want everything to look? Pass it on to the designer. Discuss with them at length what you want your brand to achieve and what market to reach.

If you hire someone to do your branding, share with them what your market research came up with. This will help steer them in the right direction. Remember, branding needs to do its job well and look good at the same time. Let them know the scope of the work you'll be asking them to do. Is it just the logo with no variations? Or will you hire them to craft your whole corporate identity?

Comparing the two, a logo will cost you so much less than asking for a whole corporate identity. However, with just a logo, you will be left to your own devices on how it's best to apply it to all your business collaterals: business card, signage, stationery, brochures, menu, and social media posts (basically, everything your consumer will touch and see). You can pay your designer on a per-item basis, but that might be more expensive in the long run.

If you go with a corporate identity, the designer or the agency will create the whole branding for you. Big agencies will conduct market tests that will usually include market research and how your consumers will react to your brand, a few variations of your logo – for when you want to place them in different items, so the logo looks optimized and cohesive in every single item – and a style guide.

A style guide is very important for your branding. It is the handbook for your brewery's visual identity. This will be what other designers will use as a guide for when you do plan to expand your repertoire or maybe even sell merch in the future. It will contain everything from your brand colors, your different logo variations, instructions on how or where to place and use your logos, and how your other marketing collaterals should look and be built. It details everything you need to do in order to stay within the lines of the brand.

Multinational companies have very strict and very thick style guides that they send to designers, marketing people, and suppliers every time someone is going to work on something that needs their branding. Heck, even Korean boy bands have their own branding style guides. Style guides have clear rules on the correct ways on how and where to use their logos. The images you'll be using related to the brand are also regulated, as well as your brand's voice.

Your brand's voice helps with your brand's positioning. Do you want to be that friendly neighborhood brewery where everyone can come in with ease? How about a brewery that caterers to the metalheads? That voice will be the one dictating how you appear in ads, social media, and packaging by regulating everything you use, from taglines to colors. You don't want your voice to appear like your brand is the vegan beer-loving aunt when your market is for surfer dudes.

Depending on the services you get, the style guide can also include instructions on how to build your packaging in regards to your branding. This is very important if you are planning to distribute your beers and you have a couple SKUs planned to come out every couple of months. It will ensure that all your SKUs will look cohesive on the shelf.

Your branding should also translate to your physical space if you have a brewery with tasting rooms or a brewpub. If your construction is already underway with a concrete and approved plan from your architect on hand, let your designer know about it so they can make your logo and your branding complement your space. The same is applicable if your branding came in first – let your architect know about it so they can incorporate the design. For example, if you have leased an old theater and lovingly converted it into a brewery, you can ask your designer to think of something that harkens back to the history of your space to tie it all together.

In a brewpub, a cohesive overall design can elevate your customer's beer drinking experience. It can create a good atmosphere that can make them stay longer, order more, and come back. It doesn't need to look monotonous with everything looking similar – it just needs to complement each other even subtly, like an accent wall here or an alcove there that can attract your target market. Remember: every target market has different tastes and preferences. Your overall design should appeal to them. If you come out with beers taking inspiration from sci-fi movies to cater to sci-fi nerds, then your space should probably look more futuristic instead of a recreation of an old London pub.

On your logo, it's best to keep it simple. A logo should be memorable, unique, and easy to replicate – it's not a signature. The best logos can be recognized and drawn quickly. And it shouldn't have too many colors – ask to get it in 2 to 4 spot colors. If you are going for the cheaper route and will be planning to get your logo made on those outsourcing websites, remember to ask the designer to make a couple of variations and to make a black and white version of it.

It also shouldn't be too intricate that you'll have problems applying it to smaller things. Any self-respecting designer will test the logo out in various sizes first and against different backgrounds for readability before they can take it to you for approval. As such, it should come with strict rules on usage. All brands should insist that their logo should have a large clear space all around to ensure brand visibility. You can't just tilt and change it any way you like just because it looks good or doesn't fit.

A lot of breweries tend to go with an artisanal and nostalgic feel, but don't be afraid to deviate from it. Just because it's a brewery logo doesn't mean that it has to have beer elements on it. You can take inspiration from various things, like the location you picked out, your niche market, or any other added ingredients in your recipe that sets you apart from everyone else. If you pivot your beers to target a group of Shakespeare-loving beer drinkers, don't be afraid to ask your designer to give you a Shakespearean logo and branding. In business, it's best to stand out in any way that you can. Attention, from anywhere you can take it, is good.

Now comes the task of creating an actual name for your brewery business. This is the name that will be on your business cards, on your delivery vehicles, on the window of your office, in all your advertising materials, and everywhere else you plan to promote your brewery business. So what are you going to name your company? You probably already have a few ideas in mind. In case you don't, consider the 5 W's of naming a brewery business.

Who

You will likely want to use your personal name in your brewery business somehow. Even if you haven't thought of this, there may be a good reason why you want to. By using your first name, it will give your business a personality, and it will make your business sound friendly. Also, if you name your business after yourself, then customers can call and ask for you directly, rather than nameless and faceless representatives.

What

This may also be something that seems too simple, but you often need to describe what your business is in the name. You want to make it obvious to everyone what your business does simply by reading your name. This may not be true for larger corporations that have a strong brand behind their name. However, in the world of smaller businesses and new startups, your business name should clearly state what you do.

Where

Another way you can set your business apart from the competition is to include the name of the community you serve within the name of your business. If you cover a specific region, then use the geographic name. While it may seem odd to use your city name in your business name when you are based in that city, customers will often see it differently. The fact that your business name mentions the area you service will gain you additional business since people prefer to deal with locally-owned and operated small businesses.

When

This is an important thing to include if you place on running a brewery service that operates 24-hours a day or has any type of schedule that is different from a regular business schedule. If your business name says enough about what you do, then it will reduce the number of questions a potential customer may have. This will make it easier for potential customers to choose which brewery service to use if they don't have to spend their time calling around asking questions.

Why

Lastly, you want to keep your brewery business name simple and focused on telling people what your business is about. You want customers to remember your business for more than your rates, prompt service, and friendly nature. While all of these are things that will help your business succeed, none of it matters if people can't remember the name of your business. You also want new customers to be able to locate your business when they search online, in phone directories, or other location searches. If your name is easy to forget, then it will be the same as being unlisted.

These 5 W's will help you get an idea of what to name your company. Once you have some ideas in mind, you can narrow the list down by considering the following tips for choosing a business name.

Always brainstorm and write down all ideas. Even if something seems unsuitable, you may end up using a part of it to narrow down the list.

You should try to keep the name short since it will be

easier to remember and write. It will also make it easier to get a website domain.

Make sure your name is easy to spell. Customers will have a harder time finding your business online or in phone directories if they don't know how to spell your business name.

Choose a memorable name so you can stand out from the competition. Choosing a name that is hard to remember may lose you customers simply because they can't remember the name of your business.

Choose a name that matches your image. For example, if you want your customers to have a feeling of loyalty, then choose a name that invites homey images.

Choose a name that makes your business service obvious, so potential customers don't have to guess at what you're offering.

Always check to ensure your business name isn't already taken. Contact your state business registration or fictitious name agency to see if a name is already selected.

You should also check to see if the name you choose is trademarked, which means you'll need to make another choice. The Patent and Trademark Depository Library can help you check for trademarks.

Lastly, write down your final options on paper and say them out loud. This will help you to see if you really like the way the name looks and sounds before you make a final decision.

Logo Design

Once you have decided on a name, you can then focus on selecting and designing a company logo. There are a few things to keep in mind when developing a logo. Consider the following tips:

Examine the logos of your competition. This way, you can avoid making one that is too similar. Your logo should stand out from the competition in the minds of potential customers.

Determine the message you want the logo to convey. The logo will imprint this image in the minds of potential customers.

Think about customer perception when it comes to color and match them with the image you want to convey.

Design a few different logos and, if needed, ask a logo designer to help. This allows you to compare the logos and choose one that best represents your business and the services you offer.

Ask for opinions from family and friends. You may find your top choice generates negative images in the minds of others. Getting a few additional opinions always makes the decision easier.

Blow up the logo image and shrink it down. This will help you determine how the logo looks on different types of marketing materials.

Lastly, compare samples of your logo in black and white. You'll want to be happy with your logo in both color and black and white.

Aside from name and logo, another important aspect of starting a brewery business is to have a clear vision and mission statement. Let's look at how you can create these.

Vision and Mission Statement

Aside from writing a business plan, another daunting task for a new business is to come up with a vision statement. This statement needs to define your business and its future. Once you have a vision statement, you don't want to let it become relegated to a poster hanging in your office lobby. The best vision statements will stay with you. With a little hard work, you'll be able to create a vision statement that showcases the core ideals of your business and provide a roadmap to where you want to take your business.

What is a Vision Statement?

A vision statement is similar to a mission statement in that it provides a concrete way for stakeholders and employees to understand the purpose and meaning behind your business. It is different from a mission statement that describes the who, what, and why of business. The vision statement focuses on the long-term results of the growth efforts of a company.

So just why do you need to develop a vision statement for your brewery business? Research has shown that employees with a meaningful company vision have 68% more engagement in their job; this is 18 points above the average. When your employees are more engaged, they will be more productive and more effective ambassadors within the community.

Since the vision statement can have a major impact on the long-term success of your business and even its bottom line, it is worth your time to develop a statement that showcases your ambition and energizes your staff.

Vision Statement vs. Mission Statement

Before you start writing down a vision statement, you need to understand what it isn't. You shouldn't confuse a vision statement with a mission statement. The mission statement is focused on the present and designed to tell people why the business exists to both company members and the external community.

On the other hand, the vision statement is a future-based statement that is meant to inspire and give direction to employees instead of customers. Both statements should be core elements of your business, but a vision statement should be viewed as the guiding light of your business.

What Shapes Your Vision?

The first part of writing a vision statement is to determine who plays a role in writing it. For a small business, it is easy to get the insight from each member of the business, which in some cases is just you. For a larger business, you will need to be more selective to make sure you get a range of employee voices heard in the vision statement.

If you are working with someone or changing your vision statement as your business grows, then consider how you can get a good cross-section of representation. One way is to host a series of workshops with key members who represent all aspects of your business. You can also assemble teams that will create alternate versions of the vision statement and get feedback from other members of the company. Individual interviews can also be a great way to encourage invested parties to speak candidly about the vision statement and give both real and honest feedback. From these methods, you can identify common themes and describe your businesses' future in words or pictures that can be translated into an excellent vision statement.

Using a Vision Statement

While writing your vision statement, you should also determine where it will appear and the role it will play in your business. This makes the process of writing a vision statement more than a simple intellectual exercise. You need to do more than simply hang the vision statement in the lobby or post it on social media; you need to integrate the vision statement into the culture of your business.

To do this, you need to view the vision statement as a living document. You should be willing to revisit and revise it. Perhaps the most important thing is that it speaks directly to your employees. Another way to help employees take ownership of the vision is to have workshops and sessions for brainstorming. During these meetings, employees should be encouraged to identify ways to incorporate the values of the vision statement into their jobs. You can then acknowledge and reward employees.

Writing a Vision Statement

By now, creating a vision statement may seem like a difficult task, but it doesn't need to be. You don't need to do a lot to develop a strong vision statement. Rather, you just need to use information you already have to guide how you'll write your vision statement. You can also look at the vision statements of the competition in order to see how you can make yours stand out from them.

When writing a vision statement, it should be concise and limited to a sentence or two. It should be something that can be quickly repeated and easily understood. But it should still be more involved and deeper than a simple tagline.

To get started, write down the largest goals for your business. Ask yourself probing questions about the core of your business. Such as what deliveries you enjoy making the most and what goals you hope to achieve. Ask yourself questions about the eventual size and impact of your business. Consider three questions you can ask yourself to get started:

What impact do you want your company to eventually have on the community, the brewery industry, and the world?

How will your brand interact with customers and clients?

What is the culture of your business, and how will it impact the lives of your employees?

After answering these questions and others, you'll have a roadmap from the present state of your business and the future. Once you have all the information, don't be afraid to dream as big as you start writing. Even if future goals seem impossible now, they may become possible later with the right employees and growth. Rather work of shaping a vision statement that reflects the nature of your business and what it aspires to become.

The vision statement needs to stretch the imagination while also providing clarity and guidance for your business. It will help direct your company and set priorities to challenge your employees so they grow your company. The vision statement needs to be compelling to all members of your business both now and in the future.

Perhaps the most difficult part of a vision statement is to come up with the wording that defines the values of your business and showcases your business identity without being too vague. A specific and unique vision statement is what will distinguish your business from the competitors.

This is a lot of information to take in. So let me simplify what you need to reflect in your vision statement:

Project five to ten years in the future.

Dream big with a focus on business success.

Write in the present tense.

Language should be clear, concise, and jargon-free.

Use passion to make the statement inspiring.

Include your business values and goals in the statement.

Create a plan that communicates this statement to all current and future employees.

To establish your vision, you will need to commit both time and resources.

Once completed, your vision statement will offer a clear growth path. It will help you determine marketing endeavors and how to focus your brand message.

The last thing you need to learn about a vision statement is that it doesn't have to be set in stone. You may not even need a vision statement at first and can put this off until you've grown your business a little and defined it more fully. It is best to write a vision statement each month and save your previous drafts to see what stays the same over time. After the first year, you'll have a clear direction of what you want your vision statement to showcase.

It is also important to know you aren't stuck with your vision statement. No matter how long you've had it, you shouldn't be afraid to change a vision statement if something doesn't feel right. You may need to rework your vision statement to be better in line with your company's direction. The main thing is to have a vision statement that is a constant reminder to your employees what the end goal is for your business.

Once you've developed a vision statement, you'll have the next difficult task of coming up with your mission statement.

What is a Mission Statement?

A mission statement is simply a statement that defines the goals of your business. It summarizes for the customers what your company does. It also explains how your business does what it does. Lastly, it focuses on why your company does the business it does. The best mission statements also extend out to show what the company does for the local community and the world as a whole.

Developing a mission statement for your new business or writing a revised one after your business has been operating awhile is your chance to define the goals, ethics, culture, and decision-making process of your business. Sometimes you will find the daily routine of business gets in the way, and reading the mission statement will give you a quick refresh by stepping back and remembering what the most important purpose of your business is.

Packaging Matters

Packaging design is one great way to promote your brand, especially if the business model you chose will have your beers appear on shelves in stores. Under the harsh fluorescent light of the grocery store filled with kids' screams and parents' sighs is the battlefield among brands. Brands not only compete for shelf space but also compete silently for the shopper's attention.

The branding across all your SKUs should be cohesive and consistent, making your SKUs look like they belong in one family. In order to capture the wandering eyes of consumers, the design of your packaging must be done well. Be it direct printing on cans or on labels of beer bottles, this is your one chance to command the attention of a prospective consumer. An eye-catching design can make the shopper notice your product, pick it up, and decide then and there whether they want to try it or not. If they buy it, it means your design is effective. After that, it all boils down to the quality of your beer. If they like how it tastes, they'll go back and buy more.

A lot of small breweries find that fighting for shelf space is a daunting task, and it's true – fighting for shelf space in supermarkets is an expensive battle. Brands would usually pay slotting fees (to help introduce a new SKU on the shelves), pay-to-stay fees (this guarantees that your product stays on the shelf), and display fees (this ensures that your product can be seen). The perfect place for product placement is, of course, on eye level, but it will cost you. Supermarkets will usually stock up the eye-level shelves with their most expensive options and relegate the cheaper one down at the bottom, where people seldom look.

Small breweries won't have enough clout or even cash to compete for a premium shelf space, so the next best thing you can leverage is your packaging design. I suggest that you go to a store just to look around and see how they display your competitors. Do they all have the same look and feel? How about their flavors? What's the trend?

What words do they use? How can you stand out and attract attention when your product is placed on the shelf?

I'd like to think of packaging design as a mini-advertisement of your product. At first glance, the most important information should be seen clearly. If you want to highlight something different about your product, you can do it effectively on your packaging. Your packaging should let your consumers know all that they need to know about your product. No one is going to be there listing all the reasons why the shopper should buy your beer, so it's all about the visuals.

A good visual makes the shopper take notice of you and pick your product up. Once they have it in their hands, all the important information should be clearly seen on the front or within the cone of vision – important information should be immediately readable without having the shopper tilt the can or bottle. The text should also be legible – no fancy illegible script that might confuse or mislead your consumer. You definitely don't want to hear complaints from irate followers on your social media.

The design also depends on how you want shoppers to see your product. Some national brands get so big that their design dictates how other brands would look too. If you want to be considered as an alternative to a national brand, then consider copying their colors and design elements. You will see other competitors use this tactic regularly in order to be considered as an option, especially if their price point is cheaper. This tactic is also sometimes used if a competitor wants to launch a new product that is similar to an already existing national brand. They would use the same colors and a few similar design elements, but still different enough so it can hold its own and not be mistaken as part of the national brand.

Also, if you'll notice, most national brands will have a uniform look across their variants in a specific category. This makes sure that when the shoppers see it, it's immediately recognizable as a part of the category of the brand. It also lets the shopper easily pick out the brand they're looking for. This is where branding kicks in with packaging design, ensuring brand recall.

You also need to know that there are labeling requirements for your packaging. Make sure your designer knows this, and you comply. Your packaging should contain your logo, your brand name, applicable regulatory requirements, net weight, flavor, and other things that you might want to call out. For example, if it's a beer and kombucha hybrid that you're launching, ask the designer to find a way to highlight the kombucha in your packaging. Your packaging design should also reflect your price point. If a design looks too premium, your target market might think they can't afford it at first glance.

And depending on your budget and the printing capability of your supplier, you will also be met with restrictions. For cans, the most popular way to go would be direct printing. This means that the can itself would be the medium of your design. Most printing suppliers will limit the number of spot colors you can use – white would also be counted as 1 color. A plastic shrink-wrapped sleeve is also an option for cans, as well as the cheaper sticker labels.

For plastic shrink wraps, you probably can get away with CMYK or photographic printing – but warping can happen when they blast the plastic with hot air to get it to wrap around the can. Most people would want their products to come out looking neat and legit, so a lot of people tend to go with direct printing. You can talk with your supplier and designer and see if your designer can find a way to make a printed label on the can look better. But remember, even though it's cheaper, you might meet problems with a sticker label on cans during distribution and display. It's not going to be as robust as direct printing would be.

For bottles, you can also opt for direct printing, but the number of colors will again be limited. Most you see on the market will only have 1 or 2 spot colors, but there's a certain appeal and feel on beer bottles nicely printed with a simple graphic. Sticker labels and plastic shrink wraps are also options for your bottle. A wraparound sticker label for your bottle will look better than a sticker label on your can. You can also have more colors since labels often use CMYK. But to make your colors pop more and look the same across all mediums, ask your designer to pick out spot colors. Your brand colors will come with their own Pantone color number – that's your spot color. Most brands will use that dominant color all across their SKUs.

As a general rule, the more colors you use, the more expensive it will get. Special effects on your label – like gold/silver foil, hot stamping, embossing, and gloss – are also added costs.

Marketing Strategies

When your branding, logo, and packaging are complete, it's time to start thinking about how to actively attract consumers. The main point here is to be able to position your brand to be part of your consumer's life or the community.

So, in short, when your target market thinks of beer, you need your beer to be the first one they think of. Consumers need to "need" your brand, not just "want." "Want" is something your consumer can live without. "Need" is equated to something essential in their life. You need your brewery and your products to be an irreplaceable part of their social calendar or the community they're in.

However, if you find a niche market where you're the first one to serve the needs to their demands, then you will reign supreme. Another way to think about it is this: you can make them think that they need something like your product and you are the only one who can serve it to them. To achieve that, you need to delve deep into marketing psychology. Yes, that's a thing – there's even a scientific journal published that covers the study of consumer behavior and the psychological study of marketing.

Advertisers can trick you into buying the products they're promoting so effectively that you're buying things you think you need but can actually live without. How do you think those big beers stayed on top for so long? They are still on top now, by the way. It's not because they taste overwhelmingly good – it's because they pour millions into not just their branding but their marketing and advertising as well. So yes, your taste and preferences can be tricked or shifted, overridden by other senses and emotion – even your shopping behavior can be manipulated.

Think about it: how many times have you craved for something you tasted a long time ago, thinking it was the best doughnut you've ever tasted, and when you finally get a taste again, sadly, it doesn't taste as good as you remembered it to be? Or how many times have you ordered something just because it looks good? Or bought something you really weren't planning to get anyway? That's good market persuasion for you.

A good marketing strategy has the ability to launch your brand to be very successful right from the start. Marketing and advertising don't just deal with the ads you see splashed across billboards; it spills over to your websites and social media posts – even your interactions with the community can be used to sell your product.

Case in point: look at the "Tom's" brand of shoes. They were one of the firsts who managed to effectively use the social cause of their products as a marketing strategy. Appealing to the burgeoning trend of environmental impact and social causes, they merged consumerism and philanthropy. They made their consumers feel good about buying their products because they are helping the community – 1 shoe given to the needy when you buy 1 pair. They had a vision, and they ran with it. A lot of brands would use the social cause for a single campaign, but for Tom's, it's part of their brand. It's easy to appear fake when you use this strategy, but Tom's smart use of their branding makes them look down-to-earth, simple, and inherently good.

Humans are simple creatures. We have our needs and wants, whether they be physical or physiological. Brands who understand their target market so clearly can play to their needs. Here are some ideas on how you can push your brand to the forefront.

People look up to leaders and authority, no matter how much they deny it. Being a leader makes your brand look trustworthy, and that makes people buy it. If you build your brand up as an authoritative figure in boozy kombucha – maybe you're the best, and you've won countless awards for your kombucha recipe, and you have decided to partner with an award-winning brewer, too – then you can use that to launch your brand as an authoritative figure in the beer kombucha mix.

Guerilla marketing is another form of advertising where you can use some kind of gimmick or surprise event that can get people talking. The bigger the impression on people, the greater and wider your reach will be. This is great if you want to open with a big bang or if you want to launch a new and exciting flavor. A good guerilla marketing campaign can drive news trucks to your venue and social media posts with no charge to promote your brand.

Integrate your brand as part of the community. This works especially well if you are a small-town brewery. You can organize clean-up drives on beaches, conduct fun activities for kids while their parents drink your beers, or even host a small live music event in a university town. It gathers people up, creating a wonderful and memorable atmosphere where your consumers can enjoy your beer.

Making your beer a benchmark for what's cool or trendy is another tactic. This is where you can scour Instagram and YouTube for influencers that you can tap. Humans crave approval from their peers, and if drinking your beer and posting it on social media is a benchmark for the new cool, then you can expect to see the younger, more tech-savvy crowd rushing to taste your beers.

Scarcity is another way of letting people think they need to get their hands on your product. Think popular fashion brands that drop their collections in secret and in limited numbers. If you deny people something they think they need, they are going to clamor to get it. In fact, this tactic is no stranger to us craft beer brewers. If you look at eBay, there's a lot of black market craft beer being sold at higher price points than what the brewer originally intended. Frankly, it's ethically wrong for resellers to sell your beer at exorbitant prices, but you can also think of it as free publicity. It tells people that your beer is so good and so hard to buy that they need to try it. Another kind of scarcity is coming up with a new flavor in limited quantities. Slapping the limited edition call-out on your beer can instantly make people want to try it.

Humans are herd creatures – we want to be accepted and be seen as a part of a community. Making your brand feel accessible and inclusive is a great way to make your market feel accepted into your brand. This is why some brands have memberships. An active social media presence is a great key here. Jump in the comments sections and interact with your market (respectfully – don't ever feed the trolls). Make badges and perks for your most loyal customers. You can even sell merchandise so your market can proudly say that they love your beer –

after all, it's also free advertising when they wear your merch.

Use social media to your advantage. In this day and age, social media reigns supreme. Having active social media accounts and websites can let you connect with your target market easier. Do giveaways and interact with your market. Doing this lets you monitor subtle shifts in your market's preferences, which you can use to pivot your brewery to accommodate. Be careful, though – just because 10 people in the comments section want a black forest cake-flavored beer doesn't mean there's already a demand. An example of social media used well is the Twitter account for Wendy's – it cleverly roasts other competitors and consumers unabashedly, and it even came out with a mixtape. Naturally, people love it. Consumers engage in threads happily, and the brand has access to multiple exposures all across the board when people retweet, like, and share it.

Events can introduce your brewery and make people talk about it. The most common events are concerts, but if you don't have enough in your budget, you can sell your beer in various events and venues. Don't be ashamed of walking around and selling your beer. Try going to various weekend markets in your city. Set up a tent and sell your beer – this tactic is great for breweries big and small, especially nanobreweries. If that event caters to a specific target market, you want to reach, having a place to sell your beer can attract first-time customers who may go on to be repeat customers.

Even wedding fairs are a good place where you can try selling your beers. If you want to see if your beer can have a future outside the US, you can consider going to trade shows. This is where people from other countries can scout for new products they can sell in their home countries. They know their markets better than you do, so if they think the beer you sell can make an impact in their country, don't be so quick to dismiss it.

New products can also drive up sales. Humans like new things – they want to be one of the firsts to taste it and brag or blog about it. Regularly create new recipes for your consumers to try. It's either you can have a few beers as permanent varieties and rotate a new flavor each month or totally change your roster of beers every month. This can get people excited to try your new beer. If you are involved in an SKU war, having 1 or 2 permanent beers on the shelves and a few limited edition ones coming out every month or so can make you stay relevant.

Use humor. Super Bowl ads are great because they are funny – Ryan Reynolds' marketing company Maximum Effort uses ingenious storytelling to make people laugh. But laughing by yourself won't do it – it's bringing people together with humor that does the trick.

Personal customization or the Ikea effect makes use of the idea that a personalized product will force consumers to take notice. This doesn't mean that you brew small batches of personalized beer. To get a clearer idea of what I mean, take a look at how Coke does it: they print various names on their cans so people can have a fun time looking for their name. It's a way to let people feel connected to the product they're holding in their hands.

Create promotions – sometimes, just a simple sale will do. Package your beers so they can appear appealing to your consumers in terms of prices, and you're good to go!

When planning your marketing strategy and

advertisements, it's best to plan for the whole year. Also, start planning before your opening or launch. Build and register all necessary accounts and websites and start posting a few months early or depending on your marketing strategy to garner attention in the lead up to your opening. It's also a good idea to hold an event on your opening and launch date at the same time. The more people know your brewery doors have opened, the better.

All About Scaling

Distribution

Distribution is going to be a huge part of your brewery if you plan to have your beers appear on shelves, locally or regionally. It's a different beast altogether, and I'd like to think they are part of the reason why craft beer is so popular – they made it more available to people. Even if giants are buying them up, there are still thousands of smaller distributors out there willing to give your craft beer brand a chance.

Most brewers will only concentrate on the production side of the business and won't even touch the logistics with a 10-foot pole, much less the retail aspects of it. A lot of brewers seem to think that when the beer gets shipped out to the distributors, everything is out of their hands. They simply let the distributors take care of promotion and sales. Even if you are already paid in full when it reaches their shelves, you, as the business owner, should also know how it's faring on the retail level.

There are a few types of distributors. First are the brand houses owned by the corporate giants ABI and MillerCoors. These are the largest and most dominant and have contracts with all the licensed retail accounts. These major distributors do occasionally pick up new craft beer brands, but they are very selective. For us craft brewers, the best option would be the small specialty distributors – they carry both imports and a lot of domestic craft beers.

A lot of them specialize in smaller handcrafted beers. Their staff are very knowledgeable when it comes to handcrafted beers and will usually go all-out when they sell your beer. There are also miscellaneous brand distributors that carry almost everything, from the big brands, popular imports, regional breweries, and non-alcoholics. Some liquor and wine distributors also carry craft beers.

There's no harm in having a few potential distributors on your list. The most important thing is that the distributor you pick who will be handling your beers in the end knows and loves your beers as well as you do. A relationship with your distributor gives you a greater chance of success. You both will be working hand-in-hand to get your beer to succeed. No one wants a slow-moving product on their shelf.

To choose the right distributor, make sure their goals and business ethics will align with yours. Spending time on the floor or marketplace is a great way of getting a feel for how a certain distributor might handle your beers. When at a wholesaler, ask for the price sheet so you can have a list of which distributors carry what brands. Also, talk to the retailers about your potential distributors. Make a note of how your competitors are shelved and try contacting them to ask about their distributors.

Here are a few things you should ask your distributor: how long will your agreement last? Choose one that will suit you and your brewing brewery not just now but also in the coming 5 to 10 years. What's their call frequency? Will they give you a brand manager just for your beers? Will they have refrigeration space for your beers? How many of your beers and product lines can they carry?

But first, before we get carried away, know your beer inside out before you try to get other people to sell it. If you are planning to distribute your beers, including a study of the regional markets and the best available distributor for you in your business plan. Most distributors, before they take on distributing your beer, would like to know more about your beer. This includes your future plans and your financial security.

Remember: there are tons of craft beer owners like you looking to ask the distributor to sell their beer. Before you present your products to the distributor, know them well first. Understand their company philosophy, goals, and what brands they have on their accounts. When you present your beers, let your potential distributors know that your beer is good and that you have enough production capacity to meet the demands when they arise, and that they will be of consistent quality. Also, tell them how it's faring now against the competitors and its strength in the marketplace. Draw up your market plan and sales projection for the next 5 to 20 years. Distributors will notice if you don't know a thing about the market.

Distributors will work hard to support, protect, and promote your brands. They have been in the business for so long that they know which beers will sell well at a given time or location, so trust their advice. Remember that communication is key. It's recommended that you have weekly follow-ups with the one handling your account. A lot of distributors would tell you to go to the floor or send someone down there and see and meet the people who are selling your beer. Educate them about your beer, how it tastes, how it's made, what the ingredients are, what makes it stand out, and what to pair it with.

If you yourself can't get your head wrapped around the logistics concerned in the distribution scene, have an operations manager on your payroll, especially if you are planning to distribute more than half your beers regionally.

Staffing and Boosting Morale

I'd like to think of my brewery as one big happy family. I know it sounds cheesy, but the cutthroat competitiveness and dirty politics at my former workplace eventually got tiring. When I started this brewery, I originally planned to brew the beers myself and have my wife and some friends help with the operations. But when we started formulating our business plan, I knew that I had to hire great people who have the same vision as mine to be part of my team.

When I was formulating my marketing plan, I knew that I couldn't be the brewer. Even though it was part of my dream, I knew my experience as a brewer would be lacking compared to the other more established breweries. So I took a step back and began handling the business side of things.

Don't get me wrong – I still brew beers myself. When you visit my brewery, you'll usually see me on the brewery floors, too. I just don't trust myself enough to come up with recipes as good as the ones my master brewer is coming up with.

The first thing you need to know is yourself and how much you can handle on your own. Ask yourself what your weakness is and hire or find someone who can help you. How many people you have in your payroll will depend on what type of business model you have and how big your operations are. I have 2 brewpubs in a metropolitan area: one near offices and another in a university town. I also sell half of my beers off-site through distributors, so I had to hire a chef, an accountant, an operations manager for my distribution, and so much more.

When you are in the planning stage of your brewery, building good relationships with everyone you will be talking to is a good way to start any business. Talk to people who know their stuff and the industry better than you do. Their knowledge will help you out big time. These are your architects, lawyers, brokers, insurance agents, designers, contractors, landlords, ingredient suppliers, and a few distributors – some distributors do end up partnering with brewers to help create beers.

Also, don't forget your relationship with your consumers. You might not be making the best award-winning beers of all time, but you still make good quality beers. Keep your quality consistent, and you'll find that your customers will keep coming back.

When dealing with staff, it's best to incentivize your employees for a job well done. Also, make sure that working for you and your business is something they can be proud of. Make room for employee growth. If you have a few assistant brewers, your business must have a way to let them grow as brewers internally until they can become head brewers, too.

Let your team know that you trust them and value their opinions, especially those on the main serving floor. They are the ones dealing with the customers a large chunk of the time. They can let you know what customers tend to like or don't like in your menus.

When you initially start your brewery, you may be able to run the business on your own for a little while. However, as your business grows, you may need to hire additional help. You will need to make sure you budget for employee salaries as well as related expenses such as workman's comp insurance, paid time off and health insurance contributions. So let's look at what goes into hiring your first employee.

Hiring Your First Employee

There is a lot more to hiring an employee than simply finding the right person for the job. You also need to focus on interviewing and training. Once you find the right employee, then you need to consider paying payroll, withholding taxes, reporting and state and federal agencies. Consider some tips that will help you when hiring your first employee.

While it is great to find the one person with skills in a variety of areas, it can be hard to find someone who can do a variety of tasks well. Rather than looking for the perfect employee, you should start out by making a list of all the tasks that are done on a daily basis or what you need help with.

Group similar tasks together and identify the must-haves for a new employee to do. This will help you start a job description so you can more effectively search out people who can perform what you need to have done. You may not be able to hire for all of your needed positions right away, but at least you'll have an overview of what people need to take day-to-day operations off your hands so you can focus on the more important items or tasks that you are better qualified to do.

You may even find that you don't need a full-time person for certain positions. You may even find out you are better off outsourcing to a company or hiring a freelancer for certain things.

Training Employees

One of the biggest complaints from small business owners is that they can't find employees who want to work or know what they are doing. Some of this can be because you are attracting the wrong candidates because you haven't defined things as instructed from the above section. But the issue may also be because you haven't adequately explained what you want to have done.

This is often the result of two primary issues. The first is that you, as the business owner, did all of the tasks from the beginning and are having a hard time letting go. This means you aren't giving the employee the chance to do the job you hired them for and are micromanaging the process, which takes away any time savings.

The second issue is that you have all the details in your head and that you only tell the employee how to do it once and expect them to do it perfectly. It is unrealistic to expect someone to remember the details. So don't be frustrated if employees need to keep asking you how to do things.

The best way to have an employee do the job you want them to do is to document the process and create an employee handbook. Write down the steps and, if needed, make a video. This will make the process available to the employees at any time that they are unsure of the steps. Rather than make them come to you whenever they have a question or guessing how to do things, they will be able to have access to the right information.

The Real Cost of an Employee

Doing the math to figure out the wages for a new employee is simple enough. If you hire someone at $15 an hour and they work 40 hours a week or 50 hours a year, then this will cost you $30,000. However, what you need to know as a business owner is that an employee costs more than an hourly wage or salary. Consider some of the following additional costs.

Taxes can include payroll taxes, federal income tax and state tax withholding. There is also Social Security and

Medicare taxes. Federal and state income tax is withheld from an employee paycheck, but as the employer, you need to pay into Social Security and Medicare or Federal Insurance Contributions Act (FICA). This is a mandatory tax. For each employee, you need to pay 6.2% to Social Security and 1.45% to Medicare. For a $30,000 a year employee, this means an additional $2,295 annually in addition to wages.

Workers' Compensation Insurance provides medical expenses, lost wages and rehabilitation expenses for employees that are injured on the job. Most states require this for all occupations, and it is an added cost to include. The cost will vary depending on the amount of payroll you paid as well as the risk factor of the work performed and the industry of your business. You should get a quote for this before you hire a new employee.

You also need to consider the cost of employee benefits such as health insurance, retirement and other voluntary payroll deductions.

Miscellaneous costs can include things like employee benefits, uniforms, training, supplies and more. These costs all need to be factored into the budget.

All of these costs will add up, and you should figure them out now before you invest in the long-term hiring of new employees.

Employer Responsibilities

When you hire new employees, there are several new responsibilities to consider. Consider the hiring process, which includes tax registration, filing reports, hanging workplace posters and understanding state and federal regulations. You are now going to have a lot more responsibilities.

Since so much goes into hiring a new employee, it can be a good idea to make sure you clearly know your staffing needs.

Final Thoughts

This is the inevitable question, and I've saved it for last: Why do breweries fail? According to statistics, there are 2 breweries opening each day across the country. Think of a brewery start-up as a rock climbing experience: you slowly inch your way up the cliff as you prepare your business plans. You can only climb over the ledge 6 to 12 months into the operation when your ledgers finally start to break even, but not everyone can hold on to the ledge long enough to be successful.

I've said again and again that the craft beer industry is very, very crowded. I'm not trying to dissuade you from starting one – I'm just stating the facts. Of course, the established ones have more fighting chances to stay in the game, but if they're not careful, an up-and-coming brewer might just take one of their slots. Not everyone can win in the shelf wars, and not everyone can win even if you have brewpubs and taprooms – you'll also be competing with local restaurants.

According to BA, the number 1 reason why breweries fail is when they finally run out of cash. That's why I advised you to monitor your cash flows. Negative cash flows for several months, even if your accounts receivable is increasing, are going to drag your business down the cliff. Numbers in the accounts receivable are not cash. As long as the customer hasn't paid you yet and the money isn't in the bank account, you'll have a hard time circulating the money to run your operations.

Remember that your sales and cash must at least match quarterly, if not monthly. Also, stocking up on inventory is okay, but keep in mind that it's also another way for your cash to flow out. Your inventory, as long as it's still not being used to make beer, is cash you can't use.

Wrong timing for an expansion can also make you lose your brewery. Opportunities are great when they come in, but you need to be able to think clearly first before jumping in and purchasing new equipment. Look at your ledgers and see if you'll have enough money for operational costs if something happens while you are upgrading equipment. Or better yet, talk to your accountant or a business consultant. If the demand for your beer rises, you don't need to clamor to supply it. You can use that scarcity to play up your strategy until you have enough money again.

As a precaution, a lot of startups like to bump up their expenses. Even if you have a brewpub or a taproom where you sell most if not all your beers on site, there will come a time in the future when you think about expansion and thus beer distribution. When you've arrived at your final numbers, bump that number up to about 50% and see if your business can still survive after that. That 50% is for the accidents or unforeseen circumstances that might happen to you and your business, like what if another pandemic happens.

For brewpubs and taprooms, it's a given that you need to scout for a location that has a lot of pedestrian traffic. No one will travel for one hour to the middle of nowhere just to taste your beer and eat in your brewpub. That plan works especially well with farm breweries. There's a sort of membership club for RVers that lets them camp and experience life in farm breweries.

So I suppose we've come to the very last part of the book, which is where I bid you goodbye and wish you well on your brewery journey. I know that everything we just talked about can be a little overwhelming – the financial statements, the distribution lingo, and the business side of things aren't always the top-of-mind skills for most of us brewers. If all you've ever wanted in life was to become a beer brewer, then why would you need to master business plans and boost employee morale and marketing strategies and stuff, right?

Now, starting up any worthwhile endeavor is never easy. I mean, if getting a business to take off is as easy as pie, wouldn't every single person in the world be a globe-trotting corporate mogul by now? It definitely takes a great deal of time and effort, especially if you're starting something from the ground up.

Still, I do hope that every topic we just covered can somehow help you on your journey – I know I certainly could have used a handy guide like this when I was starting out. Instead, all I really had was a then-pipe dream, my wife's faith in me, and the memory of dear ol' Dad. Of course, it definitely did help that I wanted to get this thing off the road, all for my father's memory. While I obviously won't be able to get actual confirmation from my old man about whether or not I did all these things right, I do know that I somehow did something with his legacy, at the very least.

Who would have thought that the last time I shared a drink with my Dad would be the last time? Gone are the good ol' days of drinking beer in pubs and talking until the wee hours of the night. I no longer have the luxury of taking a swig and clinking bottles with him or picturing we were at old-timey small-town bars that had a rusty old jukebox in the corner from the movies and stuff. And while I may no longer hear his hearty laugh echoing across the bar or watch him try to bust a move when he's had a little bit too much to drink, I do know his memory will always burn bright and fiery in my heart — and, now, in this business, I started in his honor as well.

I hope this book can do the same for you, not only in building your passions and fulfilling your dreams but also in creating your own sense of wonder and community wherever you are in the world, be it via a cold glass of beer or a colorful can from the supermarket. After all, isn't creating and finding our own little corner of magic in the world what we're here for, anyway?

www.ingramcontent.com/pod-product-compliance
Lightning Source LLC
Chambersburg PA
CBHW070642220526
45466CB00001B/257